BRITISH FIGHTER AIRCRAFT IN WORLD WAR I
DESIGN, CONSTRUCTION, AND INNOVATION

☾ CASEMATE | ILLUSTRATED | SPECIAL

C CASEMATE | ILLUSTRATED | SPECIAL

BRITISH FIGHTER AIRCRAFT IN WORLD WAR I

DESIGN, CONSTRUCTION, AND INNOVATION

MARK C. WILKINS

Acknowledgements

I would like to thank the following individuals for their help with this book: David Bremner, John Shaw of John Shaw Aviation, John Gaertner of Blue Swallow Aviation, John Saunders for his help with the Folland Notebooks, Tony Wytenburg from CAMS (Classic Aero Machining Services), Mark Mondello and Tom Polapink from Old Rhinebeck Aerodrome, Graham Rood, Curator from Farnborough Air Sciences Trust (FAST), Sarah Dunne and Karl Erickson from the Owl's Head Transportation Museum, Kip & Debra Lankenau of KipAero, Louis Clarke, Archivist for Aerospace Bristol, Fred Wildman and Rob Pyle of the Avro Museum, Darren Harbar, Ronny Barr, Michael O'Neill, President of League of WWI Aviation Historians, David Hassard from Kingston Aviation Centenary Project, Greg VanWyngarden, and Melody, for all her help with editing and graphics, and Madeleine, Robert, and Gunnar—for foregoing storytime so I could finish this book.

CISS0005

Published in the United States of America and Great Britain in 2021 by
CASEMATE PUBLISHERS
1950 Lawrence Road, Havertown, PA 19083, USA
and
The Old Music Hall, 106–108 Cowley Road, Oxford OX4 1JE, UK
Copyright © 2021 Mark C. Wilkins

Hardback Edition: ISBN 978-1-61200-881-3
Digital Edition: ISBN 978-1-61200-882-0

A CIP record for this book is available from the British Library

Design by Battlefield Design
Color profiles by Ronny Bar
Printed and bound in the Czech Republic by FINIDR, s.r.o.

For a complete list of Casemate titles, please contact:
CASEMATE PUBLISHERS (US)
Telephone (610) 853-9131
Fax (610) 853-9146
Email: casemate@casematepublishers.com
www.casematepublishers.com

CASEMATE PUBLISHERS (UK)
Telephone (01865) 241249
Email: casemate-uk@casematepublishers.co.uk
www.casematepublishers.co.uk

Facing Title Page: David Bremner's beautiful Bristol Scout 1264 taking off. Note side-mounted Lewis gun, and wrapped landing gear struts.
Title Page: Darren Harbar's image of a replica D.H.2 peeling off.
Contents Page: Sopwith Dolphins under construction in a very organized and systematic fashion at the Sopwith factory; A female factory worker hand painting British cockades on a wing.

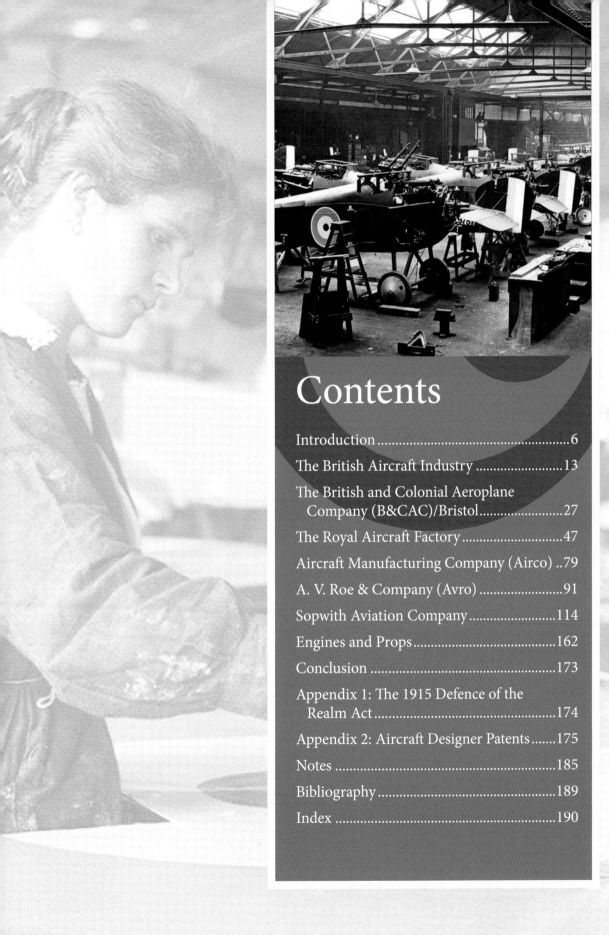

Contents

| Introduction

Aircraft reconnaissance was born out of the stasis of trench warfare and the impossible topography of "no man's land." Traditional means such as cavalry or even scouting parties found navigating the devastated landscape that included massive artillery craters, barbed wire, and a host of obstacles difficult; but this terrain posed no problem for aircraft. At last, the airplane had a practical military application. With the ever-increasing numbers of reconnaissance aircraft came the desire to shoot the opposing side's down, thereby creating the need for the armed aircraft and eventually, the fighter.

Both the Allies and Central Powers developed aircraft during World War I at an unprecedented rate. Each sought to achieve and maintain air supremacy and, importantly, each side was influenced by the other—a fact often overlooked or marginalized in many historical tracts on the subject. Innovation occurred on a compressed timeline with one power scrutinizing the other, improving upon, and attaining the (albeit fleeting) upper hand. Even within a given country, competition was fierce and sometimes perfidious. Occurring simultaneously was the notion of mass production: could a given design be built cost-effectively to

accelerated timelines given the wartime shortages of materials and equipment? And, as importantly: what materials were available in one country in large quantities? Moreover, given the exceptional rate of innovation, production techniques to produce a given aircraft had to be invented—quickly. Another important aspect was whether a particular design could be assembled/disassembled quickly and efficiently at the front. Aircraft had to be transported via rail or truck to eventually reach the fighting, so this aspect became very important to the design. Thus German aircraft tended to incorporate better modular engineering than most French (e.g. Spads) or British aircraft (lots of rigging and somewhat difficult to disassemble/assemble). Additionally, British planes had to be flown to bases in France. Why Germany did not follow suit could be attributed to early aspirations of a more mobile war, or uncertainty as to the role of aircraft once at the front; that they could be towed to the combat zone tends to support the mindset that aircraft, like artillery pieces, were simply another tool at the army's disposal.

The companies profiled in this book describe most of the major fighter-producing businesses that materially contributed to the war effort. There are some companies that produced a few fighters that are mentioned where appropriate, but they are referenced insofar as their contributions warrant.

King Edward VII, whose reign spanned 1901–1910.

Social Mobility/Stratification, Industrialization, and Aeronautical Research

The decade preceding the outbreak of the Great War was a dynamic period in British history. Although victorious, the conclusion of the Boer War in 1902 had left British leadership feeling that their imperial ambitions were on the wane. One year later, the Wright brothers made their historic flight signaling the dawn of a new age, but the British response was mostly indifferent—being a nation whose preeminence was crafted through her seafaring ambitions and accomplishments. Einstein's theory of relativity, Marconi's wireless telegraphy, the auto, etc. all occurred during the first decade of the 20th century. In Britain, the reign of Edward VII and his "bon vivant" lifestyle were in sharp contrast to the common man, whose suffering can be attributed to the very low labor wages and generally poor social conditions. Of equal concern was the plight of women in Britain—suffragettes took to the streets to try and advance women's rights. The leadership was slow to act but some did—the Labour Party came to the fore and prominent figures such as Winston Churchill advanced social programs to help mitigate the suffering of Britain's average worker and women. By the outbreak of World War I, Britain was a mostly industrialized country that focused on exports of coal, textiles (cotton), iron and steel, heavy machinery, and shipbuilding—the profits from which came to characterize Victorian prosperity.[1] When nations rushed to war in the summer of 1914, Britain's economy was immediately imperiled due the blockade that posed a threat to Britain's heavy investing overseas (£200,000,000), importation of more goods than exported, and the British merchant fleet which earned 39 percent of global merchant fleets.[2] The British blockade of Germany preceded attacks by U-boats and surface raiders, but once this began, the losses of merchant vessels and crews were staggering; totaling some eight million tons of shipping lost during the war.[3] Moreover, Germany had been one of Britain's biggest customers before the war, as had British exports of coal to Europe (which had grown steadily since 1870) and trade with Russia.

Across the Channel, the French allied themselves with Britain and Russia in an attempt to stem Germany's imperial ambitions that were strident in Africa, and threatened to be the same on the continent—building a navy to rival Britain's and a fleet of Zeppelins. The Parisian aeronautical scene was dominated by Brazilian expatriate Alberto Santos-Dumont during the first six years of the 20th century. In November 1906, Dumont flew between 722 and 726 feet in his 14-bis (accounts vary). Lord Northcliffe, an aviation enthusiast and owner of the *Daily Mail*, was present for this flight. He read the account in the *Mail* and was extremely upset, contacting the editor to say that: "The news was not that Santos-Dumont flies 722 feet, but [that] England is no longer an island. There will be no sleeping safely behind the wooden walls of old England with the Channel our safety moat. It means the aerial chariots of a foe descending on British soil if war comes … they are not mere dreamers who hold that the time is at hand when air power will be even more important than sea power."[4] With food supplies and raw materials needed for manufacturing in grave danger due to U-boats and surface raiders, Britain needed to suddenly embrace rationing and scrutiny of just what it could sacrifice and what it could not. It was in this context into which the aviation industry was thrust at the beginning of the war.

Alberto Santos-Dumont pictured in 1922. He led the aviation scene in Paris during the middle of the first decade of the 20th century.

H. G. Wells' prescient tract *The War in the Air* (1908) did little to stem apprehensions about Britain's national security—with the advent of an aerial armada, the English Channel could offer protection no more. Louis Blériot's flight across the Channel in 1909 cemented British anxieties regarding the need for an aerial defense—Lord Northcliffe was outspoken in his desire for England to advance the cause of aviation, as it had lagged far behind France and Germany. The significance of Blériot's flight as a paradigm shift was keenly felt by both the French and the British—if the Channel could be crossed by airplane, naval influence was suddenly not as potent as it had once been. The French were proud of Blériot—being a French aviator using an airplane of French design—just as any country would with such an achievement. The *Daily News* wrote:

> … a rather sinister significance will no doubt be found in the presence of our great fleet at Dover just at the very moment when, for the first time, a flying man passed over that sacred "silver streak" [the Channel] and flitted far above the masts of the greatest battleship.[5]

The *Daily Mail* described the paradigm shift that had occurred perfectly:

> British insularity had vanished; expensive dreadnoughts would be useless against swarms of relatively cheap and quickly manufactured aeroplanes; sea power was no longer a shield against attack. Men who navigate the air know nothing of frontiers and can laugh at the "blue streak" [the British Navy].[6]

Blériot was treated like a rockstar, with crowds lining the boulevards to get a brief glimpse of the man who had suddenly robbed England of the protection its people had known for centuries. Lord Northcliffe had created one of the great news stories of the time, but his ultimate goal was to leverage Bleriot's feat to compel the British government commit itself to the rapid development of an air force.

H. G. Wells, whose prescient tracts on nascent airpower helped mobilize England in favor of advancing the cause of aviation.

Lord Northcliffe, who was outspoken in his advocacy for airpower.

Blériot in his type XI monoplane. He was accorded rockstar status for his flight over the channel in 1909.

Within a week of Blériot's flight, the Liberal Government's Minister of War R. B. Haldane found himself under savage parliamentary attack for what one historian has called "the beginning of air power politics in Britain." The result of this debate was the demand for an independent air service that would eventually culminate with the Royal Flying Corps (RFC) and its final successor; the Royal Air Force.[7]

Robert Wohl wrote that, "It was one of the paradoxes of the early history of aviation that, though powered flight was first achieved in the United States, the capital of aviation before World War I was indisputably Paris. No other western city prized aviators more highly, or responded to their exploits with more intense enthusiasm."[8] British military leadership realized they had to do something—the navy would not protect them anymore, which resulted in the Air Battalion that was formed in 1911. This was soon incorporated into the new RFC and the Royal Naval Air Service (RNAS) that were created in 1912 and 1914 respectively.[9]

The military's vision for supplying its new air force with planes was very institutional—the creation of the Royal Aircraft Factory (RAF) was meant to be a locus of innovation and a clearing house for information related to aircraft design and production. Those that were a part of this organization were given preferential treatment by the government; those who weren't were not. Pioneers in the private sector such as Sopwith, A. V. Roe, and others advanced the cause of aviation using what resources they had and their raw passion for flying—had it not been for them, British aviation would have lagged behind other nations even more. During the five years preceding the outbreak, there were around 200 British aircraft builders whose production output varied widely—most of them producing only one or two airplanes. The notion of mass-produced aircraft was virtually non-existent in England at this time. Every part was carefully made by hand by co-opted craftsmen who had worked in furniture or boat/ship-building factories. After the war began, British efforts to standardize production of airframes and powerplants became problematic due to ever-changing design trends and rapid pace of innovation. By the end of the war this had changed of course, but in the beginning production proved to be a challenge for everyone involved. The British and Colonial Aeroplane Company (B&CAC), one of the largest, produced just over 200 planes between 1910 and 1914.

Blériot and his monoplane at Northfall Meadow near Dover Castle.

Regardless of the Wrights' miraculous achievement in the U.S., France had taken the ball and run with it—galvanizing their lead with Blériot's successful Channel crossing in an airplane that appeals to the modern eye; the Blériot XI had one pair of wings, a fuselage, and empennage consisting of a horizontal stabilizer and rudder. It was a tractor and had shock-absorbing landing gear. A month later there was the seminal Rheims air meet, attended by all major aviators/builders save for the Wrights. To those who attended the message was clear: patent disputes aside, the age of the airplane was here to stay.

In the years preceding World War I, flying schools were established at Brooklands, Surrey, which was then the center of activity for British aviation; and at Larkhill on Salisbury Plain where, in June 1910, a school was established on over 2,000 acres of land leased from the War Office. Military leadership envisaged training men from the Army and Navy at this facility. Many manufacturers got their start or supplemented their construction income by forming flying schools. Naturally, most of them used slightly modified proven designs upon which students were trained (e.g. Wright, Farman, Blériot)—the obvious advantage: some sales and endorsements were made on a particular company's design by virtue of the student not having experience with anything else! Using proven designs with reasonable track records also helped assuage fears of prospective students.

The Wrights had offered their Flyer to the British government suggesting a price of £500 for each mile covered with a load of two men. The sum was too high for the British and was compounded by the notion that the British aeronautical community thought they could produce a flying machine of their own. The Wrights next turned to France—the French War Ministry also turned them down due to the high price. These dealings abroad contributed to the notion that the Wrights seemed "provincial and eccentric but wily businessmen who were determined to keep the details of their Flyer secret until it had been sold at a handsome price."[10]

Despite Lord Northcliffe's support of airpower, Santos-Dumont criticized the climate in Britain regarding advances in aviation; "You English are practical, but you don't encourage inventors or beginners. You wait to reap the fruit of other people's brains." The British military remained skeptical about investing in aircraft; they were finally swayed not by developments in France but by Count Zeppelin's flight of 240 miles in Germany using his rigid airship in July 1908. The Kaiser's government intimated their intention to construct an aerial armada even more threatening than their battleship fleet. The nightmarish vision of airships "dripping death" above London as described by H. G. Wells was a clear case of life imitating art.

With the outbreak of the war, few if any planes were armed; this naïve early period of military aviation was characterized by using aircraft for reconnaissance. Aircraft on each side flew serenely by one another on their way to spot for artillery or troop movements. Young men being what they were and are, began signaling profane gestures to each other, which led to a mini arms race of sorts, starting with pistols and ending up with machine guns fully integrated into the fuselage along the longitudinal axis, such that the pilot could sight down its barrel and use the entire airplane as a "point and shoot" weapon. Regarding the rapid advances in aviation design, construction methodology, and innovation, pilot and author Cecil Lewis had this to say:

> With the exception of the Royal Aircraft Factory at Farnborough, which was a government organization, the manufacture of aircraft was then, as now a private business … Although war was a tremendous stimulus, aerodynamical data was almost non-existent. Every new machine was an experiment, obsolete in the eyes of the designer before it was completed, so feverishly and rapidly did knowledge progress.[11]

The burgeoning aircraft manufacturing industry was thus created and fostered in this context. A world war would bring the plight of the worker to a head with wartime restrictions on food, wages, and expanded hours to meet the demands of winning the war. In addition, the influx of a completely new demographic—women— would transform further the context of wartime production, as most of the men were needed to fight the war. This was not only true for Britain but all warring nations, which would empower women in this period with a purpose heretofore unheard of, giving rise to nascent notions of equality in the workplace, and women's suffrage and rights. Indeed, *Flight* magazine wrote in April 1917 that around 700,000 women were employed

A replica Blériot XI monoplane, this design, coupled with Blériot's Channel crossing galvanized support for addressing the problem of English airpower. This design looks remarkably modern; with a frontally mounted engine, single wing, fuselage, and empennage.

in the aircraft industry, and could do every job a man could and were especially good at machining small items on automatic lathes.[12] In *Flight*'s article on the fabrication of Triplex glass in January 1916, women are seen exclusively in six out of eight photos engaged in various aspects of glass manufacturing.[13] The rise of women's role in the war effort exerted tremendous pressure on parliament to allow women the vote, such that in 1918 the Representation of the People Act was passed, thus making women's suffrage a reality.[14]

Government oversight of materials and labor increased rapidly during the war; strikes were not something that helped the war effort. The biggest problem however, was that wages did not keep pace with inflation of goods and services, which led to the expansion of trade union membership, rising from some four million in 1913 to eight million in 1919.[15] Food supplies remained somewhat adequate until 1917 after which rationing of sugar, use of lower quality bread, margarine instead of butter, and consumption of potatoes rose sharply in an effort to keep British bellies full.[16]

In addition, the development of the aircraft industry just before and during World War I must take into account the availability of raw materials and supplies within England. Since England could no longer trade with Germany, a major (and close) supplier of steel, it now had to use its own steel production for munitions, ships, and other war-related equipment—the nebulous aircraft industry was last in line. The need for steel was supplemented by the U.S. but this meant using the Atlantic convoy system which was prone to attack by marauding U-boats and surface vessels. England had a limited supply of wood, which affected the types of aircraft that would be built. Unlike Germany, English designers did not maximize on new technologies such as plywood and welded steel fuselage framing—instead, they stuck with the standard box-girder/wire-braced construction that can be traced back to the Blériot XI type aircraft. Given the constraints of this system, wonderful designs were developed carrying this type of construction as far as it could go.

Finally, in the decade leading up to the outbreak of World War I, there was a growing community of scholars in Germany intent on investigating the burgeoning field of aerodynamics. There were a few epicenters of study in Germany, namely the Technical Institute at Charlottenburg and Gottingen University, as well as Aachen. At Gottingen, Dr. Prandtl and his disciples were intent on studying the performance of the airfoil via wind-tunnel experiments—an approach they co-opted from the Wrights. Airfoils of various aircraft manufacturers were tested there. Scientists at Gottingen kept the German aircraft industry informed as to significant breakthroughs—such as Prandtl's news that thick airfoils did not produce more drag than thin ones, validating Junkers' work and infusing Fokker with ideas as to his best designs and most famous direction. Interestingly, England did not embrace or digest the news from Germany on aerodynamics. Whether it was distrust or genuine disagreement it is nonetheless interesting. Britain's response to information regarding aerodynamics was the Royal Aircraft Factory, which was meant to be one-stop shopping for all things relating to aviation; be it testing a new engine, turnbuckle, or airfoil, the intent was for this state-funded institution to provide the best available information to a given question. After war broke out, study did not cease; in fact, it was accelerated based on the need to win the war. Innovations were quickly put into practice and, if successful, would be fast-tracked into production for frontline service.

The Sopwith factory with Strutters on the left, and triplanes on the right. (*Flight*, April 5, 1917)

The British Aircraft Industry

The British aircraft industry, per se, did not really exist before World War I. Military contracts, which specified fixed quantities and timelines for aircraft, necessitated that production become an integral part of the design process. Also, the state for the first time had agency to control labor, materials, and if need be to co-opt a given business under the rubric of the exigencies of war. In 1915, the Defence of the Realm Act was passed which gave the state the power to take over factories if need be.[17] In terms of production, time was of the essence so simplicity of design meant easier construction, maintenance in the field, etc. Sopwith's aircraft exemplified a paring down of the cumbersome designs that involved excessive struts, rigging, and awkward assemblies, such as those by Farman, Wrights, etc. Moreover, consistent supplies of materials became suddenly important, as did maintaining the well-being of the labor force that was tasked with building new and untried designs in a wartime context. The labor disputes and strikes that preceded World War I did not make this any easier. To add to the difficulties, most of the male labor force had to go "over there" to fight the war, thus mobilizing an eager although untried/untrained labor force at home: the women of England. Time would prove that they rose to the task; rivaling and in some cases surpassing the quantity and quality of their male counterparts.[18] By April 1917, some 700,000 women were employed in the British aircraft industry making everything from engines to completed airframes—and everything in between!

Women working on wing panels, elevators, and other components. Note the wings stacked and stickered in the rear right, and stacked on end rear left. (*Flight*, April 5, 1917)

Below at left, women using a No.9 Herbert combination lathe which precisely bores and faces cylinders for a Clerget rotary engine. At right, a woman uses a lathe to chamfer the end of a cast iron cylinder for an engine. (*Flight*, April 5, 1917)

Those that had worked in woodworking trades such as furniture making, boat building, instrument making, etc. found ready employment and training in the various fledgling aircraft companies. The rationale being that much of the skills used to produce airplane parts were the same as those used to make other things out of wood. The same held true for those skilled in metal forging, casting, and sheet metal fabrication. Covering airframes with fabric was a natural fit for women who had been employed domestically and commercially in this textile work for centuries, in all countries.

To compound difficulties, there were patents to be filed on the innovations that seemed to occur on a weekly basis in England, France, Germany, and to a very limited extent the U.S., the latter being preoccupied and somewhat "hobbled" by the Wright patent litigation that was ongoing in the U.S. as well as Germany and France. In the *Flight* issue of March 15, 1913, a report was given on the status of Wright patent infringement. The upshot was that the issue had been resolved in the U.S., and the German ruling was given orally, and concluded that the use of wing-warping and rudder together was truly a Wright patent, but that warping alone was not. The Wrights of course contested this—thank heavens for the aileron! *Flight* began a series of article updates on various aircraft manufacturers during the war years. Interestingly, they began by noting that manufacturers had two courses available to them: one to build established/proven designs, the other to strike out on their own to develop new designs—this path embracing and creating the future of aviation. Also noted was that innovation and new designs should be given "every encouragement"—this was obviously directed at the leadership in England who were initially lethargic in this regard.[19]

A photo collage of images depicting the Grahame-White factory at Hendon. Although not a major producer of fighters as compared to others, Grahame-White and his aircraft figured prominently during the pioneer days of British aviation prior to the outbreak of WWI. Collages such as these tended to underscore the vitality of British aviation companies, and painted a picture of growth and prosperity which further enhanced the notion that aviation as a business was here to stay.
(*Flight*, January 13, 1912)

A photo collage depicting the Aircraft Manufacturing Company at Hendon (Airco). Note how each photo depicts a different "shop." Due to the pusher-type aircraft initially manufactured by Airco, there is even a "nacelle shop." Note how spacious, orderly, and well-lit these shops appear when compared to others. (*Flight*, October 23, 1914)

An ad for "Croid" glue. Note that this glue could be used cold as opposed to many hide glues which had to be heated and kept warm to work properly. (*The Aeroplane*, January 15, 1919)

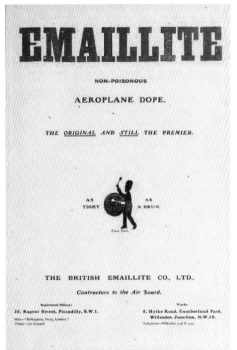

An ad for Emaillite dope. This marked a huge advance in tightening and sealing aircraft fabric; prior to Emaillite, Sago was used with problematic results as fabric loosened under humid or damp conditions. Note the slogan: "As tight as a drum" with the little drummer logo to drive the point home. (*The Aeroplane*, July 24, 1918)

An ad for Titanine—a "non-poisonous" dope. Wartime supplier's recipe for success was simple: find something that every aircraft manufacturer needs and supply at an attractive price! (*The Aeroplane*, January 31, 1917)

As the war dragged on, supplies of timber became scarcer, which led to consideration of using metals as a primary material for constructing aircraft—much debate and consideration ensued and was covered in the various trade journals. As mentioned earlier, supplies of steel for the aircraft industry were not great due to the need to use it elsewhere (e.g. shipbuilding, munitions, artillery). Very limited quantities of steel had been used since before the war in England, and after the outbreak companies like Bristol, Sopwith, and others used steel sparingly on the multiple curves on the tail feathers, wing tips, and gun and engine mounts. Still, the tried and true box-girder spruce and ash fuselage construction persisted in England throughout the war, with the industry finally considering a shift towards the expanded use of metals near the end when supplies of good-quality spruce and ash were on the wane. One could also argue that what the Germans had been doing so successfully (Fokker, Junkers) was finally making a dent in British

The shops of Martin-Handasyde, another contender before the war, but they mainly produced aircraft under license during the war. Note the more informal nature of their shops. (*Flight*, March 5, 1915)

thinking. In any event, the virtues and drawbacks of using steel were outlined by Grover Loening from the Sturtevant Aeroplane Company in *Flight* in January 1917.[20]

A fascinating and informative glimpse into the structure of setting up and producing an aircraft is outlined in detail in Stepney Blakeney's *How an Aeroplane is Built,* published in 1918. He writes without explicitly stating that he worked in one of the larger firms, and near the end of the booklet there is a drawing of an aircraft that looks very much like a Sopwith 1½ Strutter.

He begins the tract by describing how to set up a basic aircraft factory—outlining each of the spaces; metal shop, erecting shop, etc. The following is an excerpt describing how to set up the woodworking shop:

> The sawmill should next be equipped. For breaking up large timber, a 36-in. saw is useful. There will also be an 18-in. circular saw; an overhand planing machine; a thicknessing machine; three vertical spindles with a speed not under 5,000 revs. per minute; a bandsaw; a jigsaw; a grinding machine for plane irons; a brazing apparatus for bandsaws; a disc sand-papering machine; and a horizontal sand-papering machine. A four-cutter is, of course, very useful also. Also, a sensitive drilling machine, complete with wood drills. This plant will be driven preferably with 20 per cent, excess of the power required, so as to have a good margin in case of an overload. The placing of the machines in the sawmill should receive careful attention, and it is advantageous to lay out the machines on paper before they are fixed, as the long lengths of timber worked may cause considerable inconvenience when all the machines are working at once, and a considerable fall off in output will occur.[21]

The tract continues by describing efficient timber storage and location of same, ensuring that it is close to the delivery area and the woodshop to minimize wasted time and energy moving timbers large distances. Blakeney also emphasizes labeling everything for its intended purpose so as not to have the wrong types of wood used for specific components. He also emphasizes proper type of machinery with proper inspections, sharpenings, etc. to insure optimal efficiency. He continues by describing inspectors—what we call today quality control. For woodworking, he notes:

A R.E.8 two-seater reconnaissance plane being built at the Coventry Ordnance Works, February 1917. Obviously at this point, no photographs were allowed for security reasons, but sketches were. Drawing by Muirhead Bone from *From the Western Front.* (*Flight*, April 12, 1917)

He must be a skilled woodworker, used to high-class accurate finish. If you can get him, have one who has been used to pianoforte manufacture. Next ascertain if he is a keen judge of timber and knows what constitutes sap and decay, or dead wood, and find out what he would do with a pocket of resin. Would he pass it, or not? He must also be well used to, or capable of, measuring up parts with dead accuracy, hundredths of an inch count, and so does shrinkage of newly worked timber. A ⅟₃₂ in. full is better than ⅟₁₀₀ in. undersize. Also, it may save your firm money if he remembers that ash is a hard wood.[22]

It is interesting that Blakeney specifies a pianoforte maker being preferable (remember Fokker used the Perzina Piano Factory in Schwerin and its employees to mass produce his Dr.1s)—likely due to the precision involved with making musical instruments. In addition, and this must speak to an incident that occurred at his factory, the notion that a certain inspector didn't know that ash was a hardwood!

The book covers the entire process of making parts for and assembling a scout or fighter (or for that matter the same principles could be applied to larger aircraft), and it would be needless to describe its entire contents here, however, here is an excerpted series of passages describing setting up the fuselage as an example of the thoroughness of the tract:

The timber required in this case is spruce, about 1 ¼ in. square tapering down to 1 in. square to form the longerons, the length being about 19 ft. in two lengths. The spruce selected should preferably have a fine grain, which, when the longeron is in its permanent position, should form vertical laminae, as it develops the greatest strength in this position, and also adapts itself to the curves or bends required in forming the streamline contour of the fuselage. The wood might also be selected for its cream-like color, as this colored wood is generally found to have the qualities required.[23]

Next the process of selecting fine-grained 3-inch thick stock to be rift-sawn for longerons is described—right down to the number of rings; not less than eight being required for a piece of stock of 3 inches thick. The method of cutting the plank is detailed such that the result are strips of vertical-grained spruce squared to 1 ⁹/₃₂ inches to allow shrinkage.[24]

Next, the process by which a tapering jig is made for the longerons so that they will have a finished taper from 1 ⁹/₃₂ inches down to 1 ¹/₃₂ inches squared is outlined. The jig described is similar to a jig used to taper table legs. A jig for tapering struts is also described in detail along with machining of the lightening channels (dadoes), noting that a different tapering jig must be made for as many different lengths of struts in the fuselage framing, as the tapers will all be different.[25] The process of setting up a fuselage side-panel table jig continues as such:

A sketch by Muirhead Bone of the nose of a R.E.8—he was quite taken with the beauty of the propeller and describes it as "A great thing— wonderfully subtle in its graceful curves." (*Flight*, April 12, 1917)

The Hollow Structure and Aircraft Co., Ltd., Patent.

WOOD PROBLEM SOLVED.

HOLLOW SPARS

And Struts for all types of machines.

Any length, shape or section without joints.

FULL PARTICULARS FROM

ROBERT YOUNG'S CONSTRUCTION CO., LTD.,

AIRCRAFT CONTRACTORS,

CANONBURY WORKS, ESSEX ROAD, LONDON, N.

THE
Beverley Engineering Works
(Valcke & Dolphens)

Aeroplane Cylinders

Clerget   Le Rhône   Gnome

WILLOW AVENUE, BARNES, LONDON.   'Phone: Putney 478

PLYWOOD

In all Thicknesses and Qualities.

SIBERIAN & GENERAL TRADING CO , Ltd.,

1-3, Leonard Street, City Road, LONDON, E.C.2.

Telegraphic Address: "Wolsey, Finsquare, London."   Telephone: London Wall 577.

Hollow spars meant lighter aircraft which is important to every aircraft producer. This company chose spars and struts as their area of specialization. (*The Aeroplane*)

An ad for plywood and cylinders for Gnome, Le Rhône, and Clerget engines. Many manufacturers who made metal castings or machinery quickly re-tooled (at urgent request of the government) to meet war-time needs. (*Flight*)

AUTOMATIC PROPELLER SHAPER K.E.

As supplied to all the leading propeller makers.

Every blade identical.
Less balancing required.
Saves labour.
Increases output,
Write for list of users.

WADKIN & CO
LEICESTER.

An ad for an "Automatic Propeller Shaper." This was usually done by hand, but to meet wartime exigencies quality suffered nominally in favor of quantity. (*The Aeroplane*)

An ad for supplies relating to rib-stitching and taping of wings and anywhere on the aircraft where there was fabric. (*Flight*, November 28, 1918)

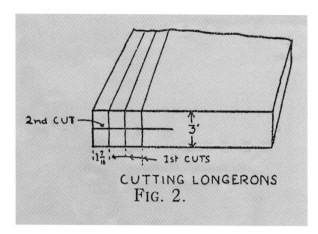

CUTTING LONGERONS
FIG. 2.

An illustration on how to cut longerons from plank. (Stepney Blakeney, *How an Aeroplane is Built*, p. 37)

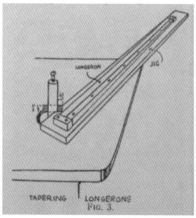

Illustration of a tapering jig used on longerons in conjunction with a shaper table. (Stepney Blakeney, *How an Aeroplane is Built*, p. 38)

The center-line may with advantage be marked in fine pencil on the longeron (cutting with a penknife in this case is not permissible). Having adjusted any inaccuracies, small pieces of hard wood about 4 in. by 2 in. by 1 in. may be fixed down by means of glue and screws to the table, being gently pressed against the longeron until their position is definite, and the glue sufficiently set. When this has happened they can be further secured by means of a couple of screws. The position of these distance pieces from either side of the center-line of the strut should be determined by the length of the steel fittings, and a small margin of, say ¼ in. each side allowed for freedom. Having fixed all these stops, hard wood turn-buttons [cams] should be fixed outside the longeron—to press it against the stops, when it is being finally fitted, not forgetting to use a piece of three-ply to prevent damage to the longeron. These turn-buttons are desirable on jigs, because they permit of quick release of longerons, struts, and other parts.[26]

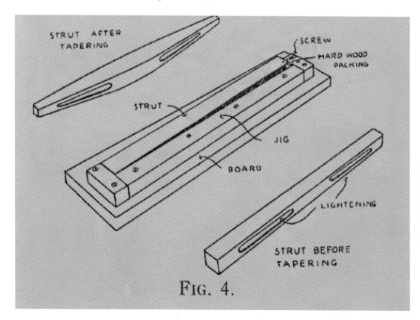

FIG. 4.

Illustration of a strut tapering jig; it is noted that the jig can only be re-used for struts of equal width and length; for each strut of a different length a new jig must be made. (Stepney Blakeney, *How an Aeroplane is Built*, p. 42)

Steam-bending of the longerons is described next which includes construction of a steam box long enough to accept the entire longeron. He notes that the steam should be about 10 lbs. per square inch, and that "care should be taken that the grain lies vertically when the bend is completed. If this process is not carried out crushing of the fibres will occur, and the strength destroyed."[27] The process of setting up continues as:

> Having got the longerons laid out on the jig table accurately in position, and all measurements carefully checked, the next thing to do will be to fit the steel fittings on to the struts, taking care in doing so that an equal amount is cut off each end of the strut, measured from the center, especial care being taken to see that the strut beds accurately and squarely into the fitting. When this has been done the strut should be tested in between the limits of a length jig.
>
> [After] the strut and steel fittings having been tested for length and found correct, the strut should be tried in between the actual longerons for fit, and it should go in with a gentle pressure. When it is in its final correct position the bolt-holes in the fitting should be very carefully marked off on the longeron for drilling; this can be done with advantage by using a piece of steel exactly fitting the bolt-hole, about 4 in. long, and slightly countersunk, like a rivet-snap, and giving the piece of steel a few light taps to mark the longeron.
>
> This having been done, pencil a distinguishing [witness] mark on the strut and on the longeron, so that it will be picked out again and put into the same place in the same fuselage, preferably use a rubber stamp. All struts will be fitted in this manner, and after this work is completed, each longeron should have the position of the fittings and the bolt-holes marked out for the vertical strut fittings, after which the longerons should be taken out of the jig and the bolt-holes drilled on a drilling machine with the aid of a metal plate jig clamped to the longeron to prevent the holes from being drilled out of center. As no inaccuracies in bolt-holes in woodwork are permissible, extra care must be taken with the drilling, and wood drills used, twist drills not being suitable.[28]

An illustration showing a a jig for obtaining the proper sizes of the cross pieces.. Note how cleats are spaced precisely to allow for fitting of metal clip fittings and cross wire bracing. Also note how longerons are wrapped in fabric where metal clip fittings are located—presumably to prevent chafing and untimely wear on timbers. Also note the "turn buttons" located outboard of the longerons top and bottom; these pivoted such as to allow the longerons to be "unclamped" and removed. (Stepney Blakeney, *How an Aeroplane is Built*, p. 57)

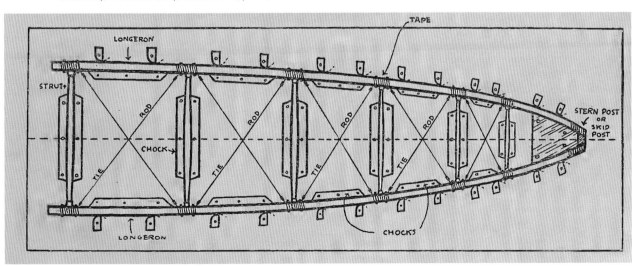

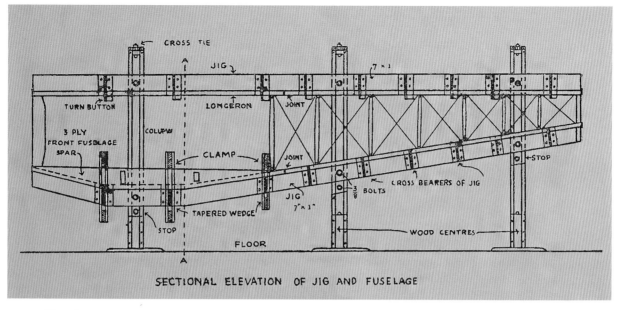

SECTIONAL ELEVATION OF JIG AND FUSELAGE

This illustration shows a setting up jig for the fuselage—note the side panels are held firmly in place and are allowed to be adjusted such that they are level fore and aft and enough clearance is provided for work under the lower longerons and not too high for work on the upper ones. This also allows each side panel (port and starboard) to be aligned perfectly relative to one another, which allows efficient and controlled installation of cross pieces, wing root plates, flooring, etc. (Stepney Blakeney, *How an Aeroplane is Built*, p. 66)

It should be abundantly obvious that this type of woodworking and metalsmithing was an exacting art, with little or no room for error. Judging by the track record of most British aircraft it would seem that these protocols were largely followed. The following describes the finishing up of the fuselage frame:

> All the various bolt-holes being drilled, the longerons will at once be returned to the erecting shop. Here the longerons, being of spruce, should be neatly bound with ½-in. India tape, tightly laid on after the surface has been well covered with glue, and also the tape, each layer half overlapping the previous one and the end secured by a couple of ¾-in. by 20 gauge brass gimp pins, after which all surplus glue may be removed with a damp rag. This binding is only required where the steel fittings are placed, and should extend about ¼. in. either side.

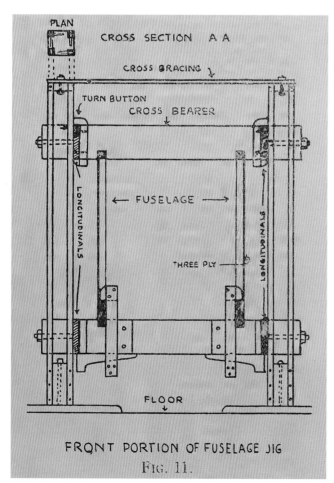

FRONT PORTION OF FUSELAGE JIG
FIG. 11.

This is the forward view of the previous illustration depicting the fuselage set up jig, showing the cross pieces that connect the two side panel jigs. (Stepney Blakeney, *How an Aeroplane is Built*, p. 67)

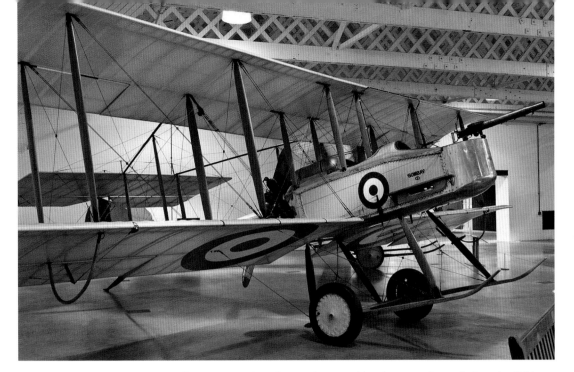

Replica of Vickers F.B.5 "Gunbus" at the Royal Air Force Museum, Hendon—similar in feel to the D.H. pushers it became quickly obsolete.

> The longeron will then be replaced in the jig and the final assembly of the rear bottom part of the fuselage will be commenced. It will be best to put in the shortest struts first and work forward, as this method will secure the ends of the longerons having the sharp curves fixed first, and also it will enable another couple of erectors to fit, glue, and screw down the three-ply at the rear end.[29]

Once both side panels of the fuselage have been constructed, assembly of the entire fuselage including all cross pieces, plywood, etc. must be addressed as follows:

> To enable this to be done easily it will be advisable to consider making a simple jig, which will ease the erection tremendously, and enable the work to proceed rapidly, and tend to prevent mistakes. For this purpose, make six portable columns standing on feet, with adjustable top and bottom cross rails and longitudinals (see Figs. 10 and 11). The use of this jig will enable work to be put in hand quickly, and when completed taken down. Reference to Fig 10 will give an idea of this construction.

A close-up of the nacelle for the Vickers F.B.5 "Gunbus" replica showing the .303 Lewis gun, and composite construction of wood, linen and aluminum.

Having completed the jig, the first thing to do will be to take the top rear portion of the fuselage and attach it to the top portion of the jig on the underside of the cross bearers as shown, and then put the bottom portion of the fuselage on the top of the lower cross bearers as shown. After which, level up the top portion of the jig with a spirit level, and then adjust the lower portion to the inclination given by the measurements of the lengths of the struts between the longerons.

After this is done and carefully checked, the struts with their fittings on them may be put in their respective positions and bolted to the longerons and riveted up, and the ash skid post fixed. Then the only work remaining to be done is to put in the tie rods and fork ends with lock nuts, and to adjust the tension on them.[30]

Blakeney's tract speaks volumes as to the exacting care that went into each aircraft that was produced at the larger firms such as Sopwith, Royal Aircraft Factory, Avro, etc., and it provides a valuable record on how to achieve high quality with a maximum of efficiency—the latter cannot be overly stressed as in a wartime context, speed was of the essence, and with the added pressure from the Defence of the Realm Act, each factory had to operate at optimum efficiency or risk government interference or in the worst case, usurpation.

Finally, there were numerous minor British fighter aircraft companies during the war such as Blackburn, Vickers, Armstrong Whitworth and of course Handley Page—but of course the latter was concerned with development of very successful bombers not fighters. These companies may have had one successful fighter design—such as the Vickers "Gunbus"—but went no further; the design either falling quickly into obsolescence due to the rapid pace of innovation, or they simply decided to focus on producing other things. There were also manufacturers that were known for other types of products, such as autos, machinery, ships, etc. but were re-tasked during the war to produce aircraft by other designers; Mann Egerton was a prime example, producing Spad VIIs for the RFC in quantity, as was Ruston Proctor who churned out over 1,000 Sopwith Camels.

The F.K.3 by Armstrong Whitworth—it was not much different from the B.E.2c, which the company was producing under license, and as such, suffered the same fate.

David Bremner's beautifully restored Bristol Scout 1264 doing a fly-by.

1264

The British and Colonial Aeroplane Company, Ltd (B&CAC)/Bristol

Sir George White was the chairman of the Bristol Tramways and Carriage Company and was also a philanthropist. His interest in aviation was not only to make money, nor was he necessarily interested in flying—perhaps he saw it as investing in Britain's future. In any event, he sent representatives to meet Wilbur Wright in 1908 and spent the following year planning his new business which he rolled out in 1910 as the B&CAC.[31] The board for the new company consisted of Sir George, his brother Samuel, and his son G. Stanley, who became managing director in 1911. It was decided to use "Bristol" as the brand name, and B&CAC as the company name.[32] Presumably White was convinced that the rapidly growing aviation business might prove lucrative in the future. The company had an initial capitalization of £25,000 which was funded entirely by White, his brother, and his son. The tram company and the new aircraft company were run simultaneously with some overlap as the first spaces for B&CAC were two former tram sheds suitable for aircraft manufacture at Filton. Moreover, the Tramway provided some personnel, such as George Challenger who became the company's chief engineer and works manager.

Since Frank Barnwell's role became central to the most successful Bristol designs, a brief profile of his development is warranted. Barnwell's father worked on logistics and finance at the John Elder Shipyard on the Clyde. The family was living at Gravesend when Frank was born in 1880. Frank's father became managing

The rather innocuous factory building of the British and Colonial Aeroplane Company. (Originally published in *The Engineer*)

director of the shipyard by 1885, passing away in 1898.[33] Around this time both Frank and his brother Harold were working at the shipyard to which their dad had dedicated his life. Harold and Frank became close and they complimented one another; Harold was more of a "type A" leader, whereas Frank was more bookish and self-effacing. Frank attended the University of Glasgow studying chemistry and philosophy; an odd combination. He graduated in 1905 and ended up majoring in naval architecture, unsurprisingly.[34]

Harold and Frank's—the Barnwell Brothers—first aircraft was a canard biplane with a 7 hp Peugeot motorcycle engine and was similar to Curtiss' June Bug, which they then modified into a canard monoplane with a 40 hp twin-cylinder air cooled engine designed by Harold, that had wing-warping and canard pitch control—it was what would eventually be known as the "boxkite" type.[35] They tested the plane at Cornton Farm, Stirling where the plane reached 25 mph and no more, needing a calculated 35 mph to get off the ground.[36] Curtiss, and to an extent the Wrights, were obviously big influences on the brothers as next year's machine featured ailerons mounted between the two planes, had a 48-foot wingspan, was a pusher featuring a 40 hp Humber car engine with twin 10-foot props, the pilot sat on the leading edge, and like the Flyer, was flown off of rails to minimize drag.[37] This plane took off steeply and stalled; it became the first flight in Scotland even though it crashed. The plane was modified with a shorter wingspan and flew in September 1909 reaching an altitude of 25 feet before it was wrecked beyond repair.[38]

Inspired by Blériot's historic Channel flight, the brothers' next plane was similar to the Blériot XI except it featured an entirely linen-covered fuselage, and Harold flew it again in 1911 and was awarded the J. R. K. Law Prize by the Scottish Aeronautical Society for his flight of one mile.[39] Frank fell in love and wanted to marry, but realized that his subsistence-level lifestyle of repairing cars and making experimental aircraft would need to be upgraded if he wanted to support a wife. Thus he applied to, and was hired by, the British and Colonial Aeroplane Co. in Bristol. Harold stayed at Grampian, which he detested so much that he closed it during the winter of 1911–12, so that he could dedicate the bulk of his time to flying, becoming a student at the Bristol School at Brooklands.[40]

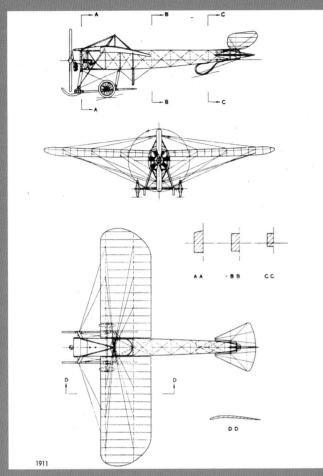

1911

A three-view drawing of the Bristol Prier monoplane of 1911. Propellers were expensive and time consuming to make, hence the skids protected the plane from breaking its prop should it experience a nose-over on landing.

An ad for the Bristol Flying Schools.
(*The Aeroplane*, April 2, 1914)

Bristol Prier type monoplane of 1911. It featured a full-flying stabilator and rudder, wing-warping, and skids on the main gear.

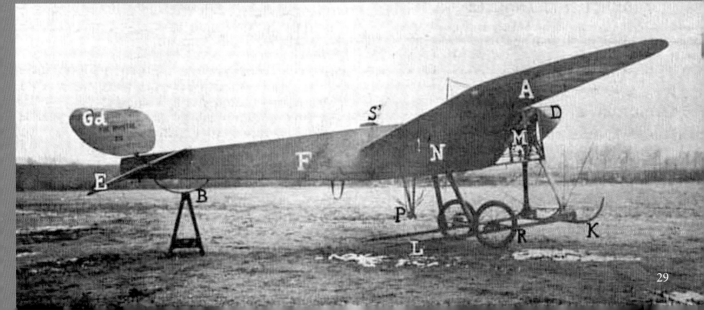

A replica of a Bristol Boxkite-type biplane built at the Royal Australian Air Force Museum. It featured a canard elevator system, ailerons on both wings, a triple rudder and a pilot, fuel tank and engine configuration that prefigured the nacelles that were to follow.

David Bremner noted that when Frank worked at B&CAC in 1911, aircraft manufacture could be broken into two camps: large firms with strong connections to the military (Vickers) and those started by aero enthusiasts such as A. V. Roe and Shorts. There were many who dabbled and there were those who pushed through adversity and uncertainty such as Roe, and those who gave up such as Maxim.

A replica of the Bristol 1911 racing biplane. Note the oversized horizontal stabilizer and elevators—his aircraft was likely very sensitive on pitch control. Also note the profusion of rigging and struts that would doom this sort of aircraft from a production standpoint.

The Bristol Type T biplane (Build No.52). It was largely a variation on the Boxkite, although it did have a forward nacelle affording the pilot some protection and simultaneously streamlining pilot, controls, fuel tank, and pusher power setup. It had a canard elevator as well as a rear elevator. It also featured ailerons; clearly visible on the top plane.

Meanwhile, B&CAC was rapidly becoming the largest aircraft company in England, churning out Boxkites, although this design was quickly becoming obsolete—other designs flew just as well and could be produced at a lower cost due to reduced rigging, spars, etc. The B&CAC design office was comprised of George Challenger, Pierre Prier, Gordon England, Archibald Low, Robert Grandseigne, Léon Versepuy, and the newly arrived Frank Barnwell; these men were all brainstorming to come up with new designs.[41] These included work on the Bristol monoplane, racing biplane, and the type "T" which was a modification of the Boxkite.

Frank had a degree in engineering, was quiet, soft-spoken, and self-effacing, with a flair for drawing—the lattermost being significant as he was hired as chief draughtsman. Frank was initially comfortable in this role, but had a burning desire to design airplanes, such that he approached A. V. Roe for a job doing just that. He stayed with B&CAC as Sir George gave him the research and design of a new airplane for the Admiralty.[42] This plane would need to operate from existing ships, have wings that could be rotated and folded back against the fuselage, hydrofoils, twin engines for taxiing on the water and for flight. At the behest of the Admiralty, Frank's office was moved to a secure location overlooking the school's training field, and he was given Clifford Tinson as a draughtsman. The resulting design was called the X3 and was tested in August 1913 by Harry Busteed, and had a 57-foot, 10-inch wingspan, ailerons, a 200 hp water-cooled Canton-Unne radial engine with two counter-rotating props. Ultimately, the project was abandoned as the Admiralty deemed the design not cost-effective.

Even though the X3 project was a failure, it did result in the meeting between Harry Busteed and Frank Barnwell while both were at Dale, where according to Busteed they came up with a sketch of a general arrangement for the Scout. Busteed also noted that the original idea for the Scout came from Harry Hawker. However Tinson wrote that the Scout was all Frank's design, and David Bremner also agreed with this as Barnwell's notebooks and drawings show no written notations from Busteed, although he may have been consulted verbally. It also seems plausible that there may have been some influence of the Sopwith Tabloid, which was being developed contemporaneously, as Hawker and Busteed communicated with one another.[43] Rather than speculate about the inception of this new aircraft, it is known that the first drawings of the Scout were recorded in Frank's sketchbook that was started on December 12, 1913 and described details of the new plane.[44] Just prior to this in November, the Sopwith Tabloid took to the air. It seems reasonable given the dialogue between Busteed

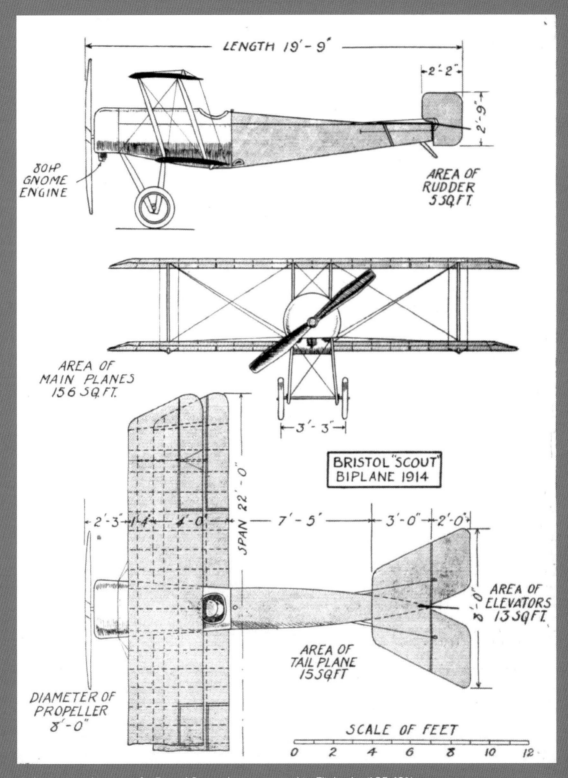

LENGTH 19'-9"

2'-2"

2'-9"

80 HP GNOME ENGINE

AREA OF RUDDER 5 SQ. FT.

AREA OF MAIN PLANES 156 SQ. FT.

3'-3"

BRISTOL "SCOUT" BIPLANE 1914

SPAN 22'-0"

2'-3" 1'-4" 4'-0"

7'-5"

3'-0" 2'-0"

8'-0"

AREA OF ELEVATORS 13 SQ. FT.

AREA OF TAIL PLANE 15 SQ. FT.

DIAMETER OF PROPELLER 8'-0"

SCALE OF FEET

0   2   4   6   8   10   12

A three-view drawing of a Bristol Scout that appeared in *Flight*, April 25, 1914.

In Profile
Bristol Scout C

Bristol Scout C: (1264) Flt Sub Lt. F. D. H. Bremner,
No. 2 Wing, RNAS; Imbros, Aegean Sea; March 1916.

and Hawker noted that the basic design path or arrangement of the Tabloid may have been known at B&CAC. Moreover, the press went wild with news of the new Sopwith plane which likely compelled other companies to come up with something similar—a small, fast, single-bay tractor scout—especially since the War Office ordered 40 Tabloids by early 1914.[45]

The general construction of the Scout (works sequence 206) is not earth-shattering. The 22-foot wings in planform were rectangular with ailerons on both upper and lower planes, and the airfoil was likely taken by extension from Nieuport aircraft.[46] Also similar to Nieuport was the "horseshoe"-shaped cowling although the new "baby biplane" had a blunter-forward cowling face.[47] It was powered by a 80 hp Gnome rotary, and had a conventional horizontal stabilizer and elevator, and also like the Nieuport—a full-flying rudder. It was tested by Harry Busteed at Larkhill on February 23, 1914, and it reached a top speed of 95 mph.[48] In April, it was returned to Filton for incorporation of modifications slated after testing was completed. These included increased span, chord, and dihedral of wings, shortened ailerons and a larger rudder—obviously the roll rate was too high and the rudder authority too low. Finally, it was given a full rounded cowling. All of these modifications coalesced to give the resultant aircraft a top speed of 97.5 mph when it was again tested this time at Farnborough in May 1914.[49] The two Scouts (#229, 230) were delivered to the Royal Flying Corps at Farnborough in late August, and were given official service numbers of 633 and 648. Further modifications were then made including doubled flying wires and improved interplane bracing, wider track undercarriage, a bulbous new cowling, and bowed wing-tip skids were fitted under the interplane struts.[50] Interestingly, the Scout had no provision for an effective armament which was largely due to the role envisaged for aircraft at this juncture—reconnaissance

Prototype of the Bristol Scout at the Aero & Marine Exhibition, Olympia, London, March 1914.

David Bremner: Building a Bristol Scout

David Bremner started building his Bristol Scout in 2008, and it took to the air for the first time on July 9, 2015, almost exactly 100 years after the original. He had this to say about the project:

Theo suggested it, somewhat idly, and we were at a time in our lives when we had enough time to start the research. If Grandad had flown a Camel, we wouldn't have bothered because there are plenty of others around. If he'd flown a Short 184 it would have been beyond our means. But he flew the Scout which is the perfect project for home building. If I hadn't gone to the RAF's library in London to look at Barnwell's original notebook, I wouldn't have been put in touch with the guy in Houston who had high quality scans of about 90% of the factory drawings. And so on. The decision points were in late 2007 when we had to decide whether to start spending money on materials, and then the engine from TVAL stopped us; coming to a grinding halt.

My Grandad kept copious records, probably because he wasn't out there long enough to have suffered from stress (though he was off all work for nine months with dysentery / malaria / trench fever) and it was a huge privilege to read his log book and get to know the 23-year-old, when I knew him from 60–90.

But the trip to Greece and France was entirely serendipitous thanks to a contact with historian Paschalis Palavouzis, who is related to Panos

Georgiadis, who runs the Kavala airshow, and it was through them that we got funding and the whole thing happened.

The flight itself was horrible—the airstrip wasn't prepared when we got there; the weather started to deteriorate and in the end there was only the one morning at dawn out of the whole week when it was possible to fly. Even then it was so bumpy I was being splashed with fuel from the vent pipe on the petrol tank, so my idea of flying round for an hour and getting up to 4,000 ft to try and see what Grandad saw went out of the window and I did 10 uncomfortable minutes and got down before the wind changed direction!

So there was relief that we'd got it done, but not a huge amount of romance.

I think the lasting pleasures I've had have been getting to know Grandad, being able to share the journey with Theo and Sue, getting to know the astonishing people at the Shuttleworth Collection and being allowed to display with an amazing collection of pilots, and—in 2018 particularly—getting to share the story with so many people at static events.

A drawing showing forward framing of the Scout. (Image courtesy of David Bremner)

and observation. Lanoe Hawker devised an interesting mount for a Lewis gun which fired down and outboard to avoid the prop; he was able to shoot down three German two-seaters in this fashion.[51] Likely following the French Nieuports, an overwing mount for the Lewis gun became standard for the Scouts by spring of 1916.

The last surviving Bristol Scout was rescued by Leo Opdyke of Poughkeepsie, New York—a longtime WWI aviation enthusiast. Leo had no workshop, no experience, not many flying hours, but began diligently and patiently working out of his garage in Rochester, NY, later moving to Poughkeepsie. Drawings came from the Smithsonian Institution and it took him approximately 15 years to complete his Scout—being ready to fly in 1986. It was transported to the Old Rhinebeck Aerodrome, and before taking off, Cole Palen suggested he check the magneto on the 80 hp Le Rhône; intimating that due to its age it might not be in the best shape; after 20 minutes in the air it quit, with Leo ending up in the trees.[52]

David Bremner in the cockpit of his rebuilt Scout 1264 showing uncovered fuselage framing and completed wing panels, struts and rigging. (Image courtesy of David Bremner)

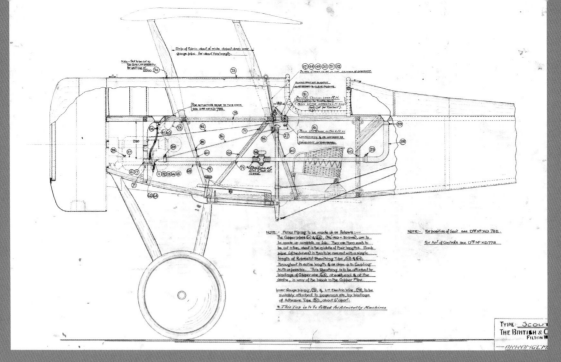

A drawing showing the forward construction plan for the Bristol Scout. (Image courtesy of David Bremner)

David Bremner's beautifully finished Bristol Scout seen doing a fly-by. (Image courtesy of David Bremner)

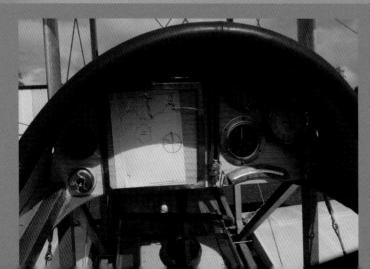

The Spartan cockpit of Bremner's 1264 Scout. (Image courtesy of David Bremner)

Archival image of RNAS Scout D's cockpit—note the dual Lewis guns flanking the cockpit. No provision had been made for armament for the Scout and as such it was added as an afterthought; no one had envisaged that scouting aircraft would be trying to shoot each other down.

The Bristol M.1A "Bulldog"

Regarding the M.1A, J. M. Bruce, prolific author on WWI and WWII aircraft, wrote that this was Barnwell's solution to high performance and optimum view for the pilot. The Bristol was, in Bruce's opinion, more worthy of development, yet it saw limited production and had a nominal if not obscure combat record. This may have been the result of the ban on monoplanes mandated by the British in favor of biplanes for a needlessly long time.[53] The M.1A looked similar to the Morane Saulnier N "Bullitt" of 1914/15 which could have been an influence on Frank Barnwell.

The Bristol M.1A was powered by a 110 hp Clerget 9Z engine. The prototype was rolled out in July 1916 as works sequence 1374. It had a very streamlined airframe which was rounded in section—as far as stringers and formers would allow. What is particularly interesting and noteworthy about the fuselage, is the apparent use of formers that were made either from stack-laminated spruce or steam bent as they are very thin in width and depth. They could not have been sawed from flat stock to shape as this would be weak and wasteful especially during a time when aircraft timbers were allegedly getting scarce. Likely each of these frames would have either been steam-bent (in the case of steaming) or cold laminated and clamped to a master re-usable set of forms.

Another view of 1264 with Bremner in the cockpit. (Image courtesy of David Bremner)

A Bristol M.1A. (Image courtesy of Greg VanWyngarden)

There may also have been a master fuselage "plug" as with the Pfalz type fuselages to which these formers could have been clamped. In either case, there would have needed to be something along these lines to facilitate efficient production. The completed formers were fitted to the standard box-girder, wire-and-turnbuckle-hardened interior construction, much in the way the fuselage of the Nieuport 28 was, but with the added advantage of being—I would imagine—much lighter. Also, both the Nieuport 28 and the Morane Saulnier N featured ply formers perforated by lightening holes that were in turn attached to vertical and athwart struts, thus the system employed on the M.1A was a unique solution to the problem. All of these types of aircraft (N28, MSN, and the M1) had one thing in common: the interior box-girder core structure was the strength of the fuselage, with the formers and stringers forming the aerodynamic fairing of the finished fuselage.

The wings were fastened to the upper longerons, and in planform were a sweeping elliptical shape that prefigured those of the Spitfire and more modern aircraft. The construction of the wings was comprised of two main spruce spars; the forward one shorter than the aft due to the shape of the wing, and standard rib formers, and ailerons. The wings were supported by means of RAF wires above and below the wings (flying wires were doubled), terminating on the lower longerons below, and a superstructure of streamlined tubing above. Cantilevered wings (like Fokker or Junkers aircraft) would have made this a truly formidable weapon but, alas, this was not a direction pursued by England at this time.[54]

A Morane-Saulnier Type N Bullet.

A Morane-Saulnier Type N Bullet with fixed machine gun at Breuil-le-Sec aerodrome February 2, 1916.

The fairings of the fuselage Bruce notes required more man hours than a slab-sided structure but he claims this would have been offset by the savings in wing-building time (due to it being a monoplane). Of course, the E.III had the best of both worlds.[55] Capping off an already slippery fuselage was a large shallow depth spinner—looking like a salad bowl—that covered most of the front face of the Le Rhône, as well as maybe a third of the prop. The M.1A was test flown on July 14, 1916 at Filton by F. P. Raynham, reaching a top speed of 132 mph. It was again tested at Central Flying School at Upavon later that month including 50 lbs. of ballast for a machine gun, plus 17.5 gallons of fuel split among three tanks.[56]

It reached 128 mph at 5,400 feet, 120 mph at 9,300, and 110.5 mph at 15,000 feet. Best rate of climb was achieved at 70 mph. The flight report noted the machine was tiring to fly, that it required a good pilot, with a moderate ease of handling. The plane was noted as being nose heavy in a glide, with tendency to pull to the right with engine on. It is surprising that there was no mention of the plane's excellent visibility for the pilot looking up; he couldn't see anything looking down.[57]

A replica of Morane-Saulnier Type N 5191 in the workshop of the North East Land, Sea & Air Museums (NELSAM), Sunderland.

A rare image of a Bristol M.1 with linen covering removed showing light and streamlined fuselage framing and stringers. (Image courtesy of Greg VanWyngarden)

Another view of the M.1 looking aft. Note the internal box-girder construction to which light formers and stringers are attached. (Image courtesy of Greg VanWyngarden)

The cockpit view of the M.1C displayed at the Royal Air Force Museum, Hendon. The characteristic wicker seat is present and an ad hoc arrangement of instruments. (Image courtesy of Greg VanWyngarden)

Another view of the M.1C's cockpit displayed at the Royal Air Force Museum, Hendon, showing the stick, rudder bar, compass, mixture control, and dual magneto switches. (Image courtesy of Greg VanWyngarden)

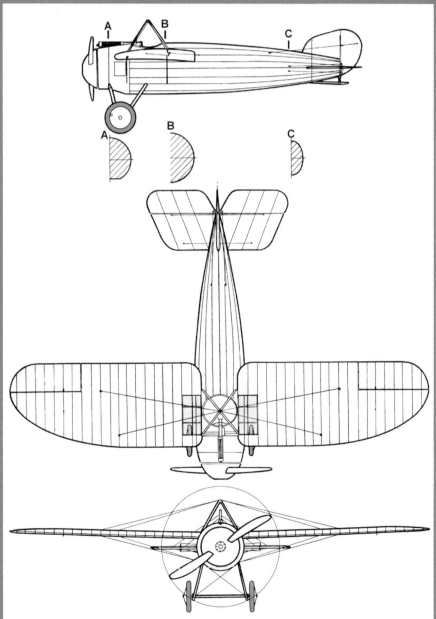

Line arrangement diagram of the Bristol M.1 Bullet.

A replica Bristol M.1C
C4918 G-BJWM
in the care of The
Shuttleworth Collection.

In spite of the limited downward view, the War Office continued to test the M.1A and some M.1Bs were sent overseas for combat testing. Bruce stated that "fear of landing difficulties in the small French airfields prompted the curious decision to send the aircraft to the Middle East in June 1917—much to the chagrin and furor of British pilots on the Western Front; who craved a superior weapon such as the M.1A which had no vices, great field of vision upward and forward, maneuverability, and a forward-firing machine gun."[58] As Major Oliver Stewart was quoted as saying: "Bristol Monoplane: These were the words that brought hope and encouragement to many a war pilot."[59]

There is only one original M.1C in existence—the Red Devil flown by Harry Butler, currently on display in Minlaton, South Australia.

Captain Harry Butler's "Red Devil," the only surviving original M.1C on display in a purpose-built museum at Minlaton, South Australia.

The Bristol F.2B "Brisfit"

Perhaps one of the most amusing stories about re-purposed aircraft is the story of one Mr. Boddington who at the conclusion of the war bought six F.2B fuselages for £25—for firewood! He then changed his mind and used them as roof trusses for his barn! These were eventually discovered by the right pair of eyes and one went to the RAF or Imperial War Museum, the other went to Canada and by way of Roger Freeman ended up in Fred Murrin's hands. Mr. Murrin completed this restoration for a private client.

The RFC noted the need for a replacement for the B.E. by fall of 1915. The new aircraft would have to be a sturdy reconnaissance aircraft that had enough firepower to defend itself—unlike the poor B.Es. The R.E.8 was a direct result of this need, and although an unsatisfactory design in the end, thousands were built. While the R.E.8 was being developed at RAF, Frank Barnwell was working on a design at Bristol resulting in the R.2A which was a two-seater biplane powered by a 120 hp Beardmore engine, which was replaced by R.2B featuring the 150 Hispano-Suiza engine and unequal span wings.[60] Both designs featured the terminus of the fuselage aft a horizontal knife edge so to speak, which afforded the gunner a good field of view. To compensate for the lack of vertical depth of yielded by a traditional fuselage with a vertical post that would then extend upwards, the R.2s had a large portion of the vertical fin below the fuselage as well as above. In addition, the lower plane was mounted 12 inches below the fuselage's lower longerons, which afforded the pilot excellent downward visibility, and the gunner the ability to fire over the upper wing.[61]

In Profile
Bristol F.2B

Bristol F.2B Fighter: (B1330) No. 39 (HD) Squadron, RAF; North Weald, UK; March 1918.

48 Sqn Bristol F.2A A3323 downed April 11, 1917—Lothar von Richthofen's second victory. (Image courtesy of Greg VanWyngarden)

The fuselage of the big powerful fighter was standard box-girder construction, with most of the airframe made from spruce of 40mm forward tapering to 20mm at the tail, with the forward ⅗ths of the lower longerons made from ash for extra strength, and hardened with steel tie-rods and fittings. The gunner's compartment was defined by means of plywood panels, and an arched steel tube support spanning the upper longerons forward of the pilot's cockpit to secure the aft end of the Vickers gun. Steel tube was also used to secure the aft end of the engine to the longeron/strut frame. The forward portion of the fuselage turtle deck was made from aluminum sheet, and the rest was laced linen, in the manner of most British planes—allowing these panels to be unlaced and removed for servicing/inspection of the wooden airframe, associated fittings, and control cables.

The wings were made in the conventional fashion (as was every other aircraft in the war save for Fokker and Junkers), and comprised of two spruce spars over which 14 rib formers were positioned, and between which two riblets tied the leading edge to the forward spar. This practice was widespread, and allowed for a more rigid entry for the airfoil and consequently made a more efficient lifting surface and a stronger one as well. The 1st, 5th, 8th and 11th were compression ribs (solid between spars except for 1st which is totally solid).[62]

Bristol F.2B of No 48 Squadron, with starboard aft fuselage (linen) panel removed, showing straightforward box-girder construction. What is not apparent in the photo is the fine attention to detail and resulting strength of its construction. For example, the splices on the longerons were scarfed and riveted to insure they would never come apart under load.

The F.2B on display at the Royal Air Force Museum, Hendon. Note the lightness of the rib webs, also notice the whipping of the main spars between frames. The ends of the interplane struts are also tightly wrapped in fabric to ensure that the ends of the timbers would not split under the stress of combat.

The empennage was made from composite steel tube and spruce construction; the rudder was entirely steel ($^3/_4$ inch LE and $^3/_8$ inch TE), and the outline of the vertical fin was also steel with spruce formers, just as was the elevator and horizontal stabilizer.[63] The incidence of the horizontal stabilizer was variable, which had become a hallmark of British aviation industry during the war.

When the 190 hp Rolls-Royce Falcon I became available Frank drew a third design that incorporated the earlier R.2 models but with a revised engine area and a fixed forward-firing Vickers gun that was made possible by synchronizing gear that was then available. The new aircraft had a distinctive fighter-like quality, so much so that it was given the name of F.2A. The War Office liked it such that they placed an order for two prototypes A3303 and A3354, the first of these making its test flight on September 9, 1916. The second of the prototypes had a 150 hp Hispano-Suiza "Hisso" fitted to it with a circular radiator. It became quickly apparent that the A3303 to which shutters had been fitted on either cheek to allow cooling, obstructed the pilot's field of vision. The nose was redesigned with no shutters/louvres incorporated an ovoid radiator.[64]

Official trials were conducted at Upavon on October 16 and 18, 1916, using both a 4-blade and 2-blade prop. It was then fitted with a Scarff No. 2 gun ring mounting for the aft cockpit, and an Aldis sight for the forward-firing Vickers. The 50 production F.2As had the 190 hp Falcon I, and delivery of these aircraft began just before Christmas of 1916. Deployment and use of these aircraft was withheld until the beginning of the battle of Arras.[65]

The F.2B D8096 of The Shuttleworth Collection doing a fly-by.

Shuttleworth's F.2B D8096 in flight over the English countryside. (Image courtesy of Darren Harbar)

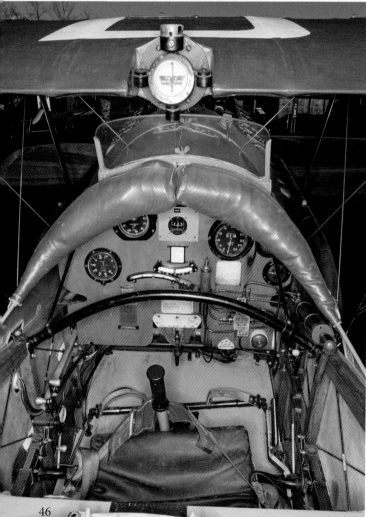

Two hundred additional models, A7101–A7300 were ordered in November, but these aircraft differed from the original 50 in that the lower wing attachment system was replaced by a fully covered center section, with the upper longerons sloping downwards from the rear of the pilot's cockpit which facilitated the re-modelling of the forward fuselage, giving the pilot a better forward view. In addition, new horizontal tail surfaces were designed and implemented that featured a reduced chord and increased span. The newly modified aircraft was designated the F.2B or "Bristol Fighter."[66]

The cockpit of the F.2B. Note the compass let into the trailing edge of the upper plane which reduced magnetic interference. (Image courtesy of Darren Harbar)

The Royal Aircraft Factory

By 1911, British leadership finally acknowledged the ascendancy of aviation by forming the Royal Balloon Factory at Farnborough which was soon renamed the Royal Aircraft Factory (RAF). It was intended to be an epicenter for excellence and innovation for the burgeoning British aviation industry. Like Gottingen in Germany, it was also meant to be a resource for the nation's airplane designers and manufacturers.

The Shuttleworth S.E.5a. (Image courtesy of Darren Harbar)

The first plane built there was created from the remains of a wrecked Blériot monoplane reworked as a canard biplane, and was designed by the RAF's first chief designer Geoffrey de Havilland. It was called the S.E.1 (short for Santos Experimental 1), a nod to Santos-Dumont who had popularized canard-style control surfaces.[67]

Mervyn O'Gorman was superintendent of the RAF from 1911 to 1916. He and de Havilland continued to design new planes which were experimental and tentative. O'Gorman then decided to rename the planes there to B.E. for tractors (Blériot Experimental) and F.E. for pushers (Farman Experimental).

The B.E.2

RAF staff were anxious to create a new type of airplane although they had no permission to do so until January 1911—after which they went overboard with their new-found freedom—transforming, as mentioned, a damaged Blériot monoplane they had received in 1910 into the bizarre and awkward S.E.1.[68] The same liberal interpretation of "reconstruction" was applied to a Voisin they received in 1911 and was given the designation of B.E.1 (Blériot Experimental). It was a biplane of unequal span, and originally had no dihedral, with wing-warping and minimal rigging. The fuselage was of braced box-girder construction with a cambered turtle deck aft of the rear seat. It had an uncowled Wolseley V-8 engine with the radiator mounted on the faces of the forward cabane struts, thus effectively blocking the forward field of vision. Elevators and full-flying rudder were made from steel tubing, with the horizontal stabilizer of wood and steel. It featured mufflers on the engine and as such was fairly quiet, and was given the first certificate of airworthiness by S. Heckstall-Smith, Superintendent, Army Aircraft Factory, March 14, 1912, South Farnborough.[69]

Over the course of the lifespan of The B.E.1, various modifications were made including an enlarged tailplane and a modified gravity tank, and a slight increase in dihedral. The original Wolseley engine was eventually replaced by a 60 hp V-8 (air-cooled) Renault which improved forward visibility.

In February 1912, a second aircraft was built—the B.E.2. It featured a 70 hp Renault engine, wings of initially equal span, and was first seen at Brooklands on February 24, 1912.[70] Two more were built in the B.E. series (B.E.3, B.E.4) but had Gnome rotaries, and the fifth had 60 hp ENV engine.[71]

The War Office had announced a competition for military airplanes in the late summer of 1912—the goal was simple: pick the best all-around airplane for the Royal Flying Corps. It was a seminal moment in the British military aviation, with 31 aircraft from 20 manufacturers in attendance. As Mervyn O'Gorman was a judge, all aircraft from the RAF were ineligible for the competition. However, the War Office liked the B.E. aircraft, so the work around was to give a contract to Vickers to build four B.E.2 aircraft on May 31, 1912. The trials were held in August at Larkhill, and although not being considered at the competition, de Havilland did demonstration flights in parallel, showing everyone that the B.E. was the best airplane at the event. The winner of the contest per se was S. F. Cody, whose biplane was not a serious contender for production due to its inherent complexity.

Interestingly, the Royal Aircraft Factory only produced five B.E.2as (in 1913). This is important insofar as the factory received strong public criticism for receiving preferential treatment by the British government. J. M. Bruce felt that the diatribes against the Royal Aircraft Factory were "strongly biased, ill-informed and largely inaccurate, and occasionally naive in its blatant and clamorous anxiety to condemn at all costs."[72] The bulk of B.E.2s were contracted to other companies, and the earliest production models were characterized by unequal span wings, but these would be changed to equal spans on the B.E.2as as was a revised fuel system—these began being delivered in 1913.[73]

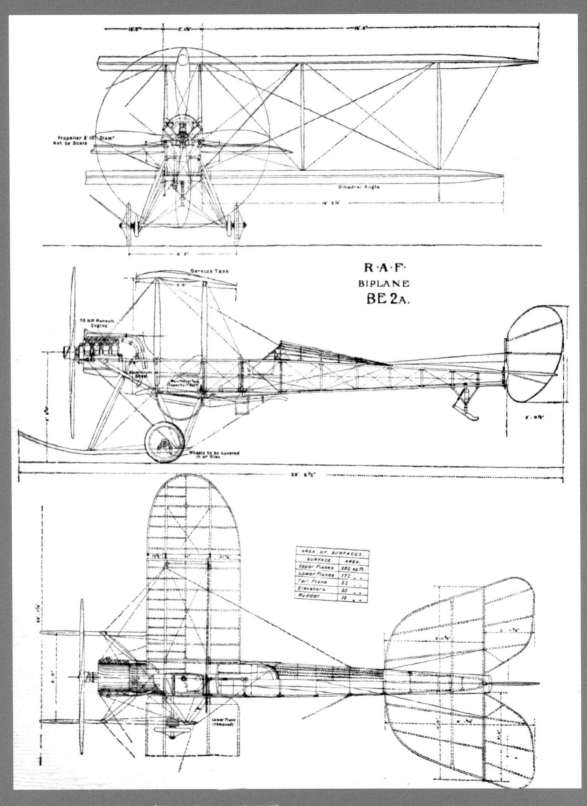

A drawing of the B.E.2a. (*Flight*, October 18, 1913)

A replica of B.E.2a No.471 at Montrose Air Station Heritage Centre, Angus, Scotland. Note the absence of ailerons indicating wing-warping.

The Royal Aircraft Factory, as a locus for the latest data on all things related to aviation, experimented with B.E.2as, conducting tests on various types of undercarriages (which informed the gear on the F.E.2, R.E.7 and some B.E.2cs), and stability tests.

At one time, a B.E.2a fitted with this form of undercarriage was also provided with a set of experimental interplane struts, that had appreciably increased chord at their upper ends. These "fin struts" were designed by E. T. Busk as part of his experiments in the investigation of aircraft stability.[74]

Early in 1914, the B.E.2a was re-designed with an improved cockpit and deeper turtle deck on the fuselage that afforded the crew great safety and comfort. The elevator and rudder controls were also revised. Sadly, wing-

An early production model of the B.E.2.

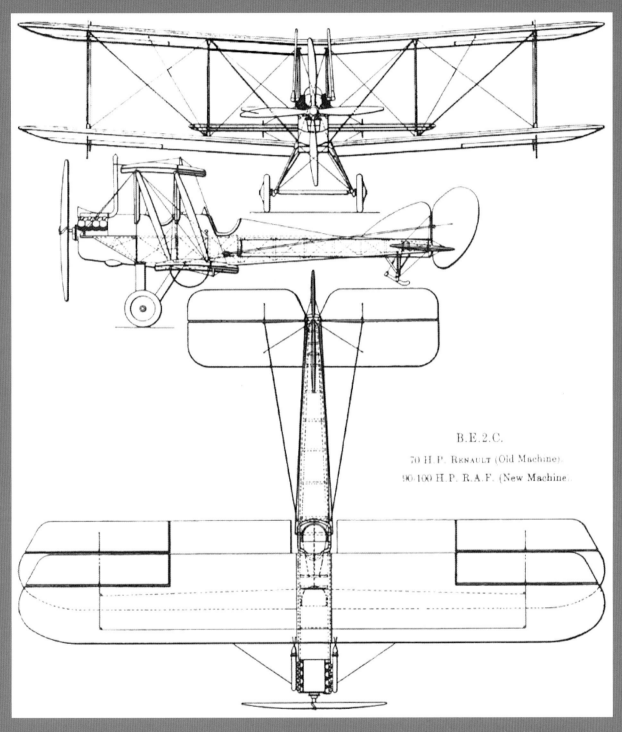

B.E.2.C.

70 H.P. RENAULT (Old Machine).

90-100 H.P. R.A.F. (New Machine).

A three-view drawing of the B.E.2c, note the presence of ailerons on this model; a considerable improvement over the original wing-warping.

A B.E.2c with covering partially removed in the Canada Aviation Museum, Ottawa; note the 90° bend in the exhaust stacks which kept the engine fumes well over the pilot and observer's heads.

warping was retained as was the 70 hp Renault engine. The B.E.2a and 2b remained in service well into 1915, but by the end of August, their use was almost over, with only five still in service with the R.F.C. in France.[75]

Finally, the B.E.2 was conceived as a purely reconnaissance aircraft; no provision was envisaged or planned for any type of defensive let alone offensive armament. Events evolved rapidly in the air, and with the advent of the Fokker E series of monoplanes the notion of the first point and shoot weapon became a reality. The mistake leadership made was in keeping the B.E. in service as long as they did.

In 1913, Brigadier General David Henderson, commander of the military wing, mandated that no aircraft of the Royal Aircraft Factory could be powered by engines that exceeded 100 mph as he believed that no "useful flying" could be accomplished at a greater speed.[76] This obviously spoke to the role he envisaged for the airplane which was strictly reconnaissance—seemingly he was directly informed by the B.E. series of aircraft; it was a fateful decision.

In contrast, Charles Rumney Samson, commander of field operations for the RNAS, believed that aircraft could play an offensive role in combat, and should not be relegated to reconnaissance alone. He led by example and took his men on bombing raids on Zeppelin bases.[77]

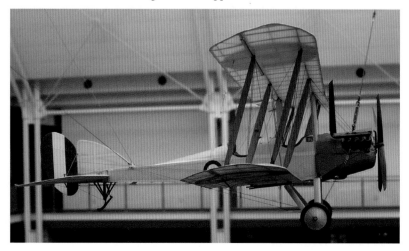

The B.E.2c at the Imperial War Museum in London.

A Fokker E.II of late 1915 which featured wing-warping and most importantly: a machine gun that was synchronized to fire through the propeller without hitting it.

However, in order to make aircraft truly offensive, they had to be able to pursue and shoot down the enemy. One of the biggest challenges facing the allies was the lack of a workable and reliable interrupter/synchronizing gear which allowed the machine gun to be fired through the propeller, and for the pilot to sight down its length. Garros attempted a crude remedy by fixing metal plates to the aft sides of the prop of a Morane monoplane to protect it from being shot off when bullets hit. This solution was imperfect at best. What made the Fokker Eindecker such a formidable weapon was its synchronizing gear that allowed it to fire through the prop safely and become the first true "point and shoot" weapon. The slow delicate B.E.2s were sitting ducks for the Fokker Eindeckers with the synchronized forward-firing machine gun—it was a game changer. Blame for the carnage was aimed at the Royal Aircraft Factory and this rage had a face: Noel Pemberton Billing, who founded the Supermarine flying boat works in Southampton (and then sold it without building a single plane).[78]

Pemberton Billing coined the phrase "Fokker Scourge" and in his address to parliament he blamed the poor designs of the Royal Aircraft Factory and the government's unwillingness to support other manufacturers resulting in effect a monopoly.[79] Lord Northcliffe and Charles Grey added their voice to Pemberton Billing's, and accused the War Office of giving the RAF preferential treatment. Icing on the cake: Pemberton Billing told the House of Commons a quote by Lt. Col. Walter Faber that "airmen were being murdered rather than killed thanks to the inadequacy of their airplanes."[80]

Fokker Eindecker, built by Achim Engels of Fokker Team Schorndorf in Germany. (Fokker Team Schorndorf)

Fokker Eindecker. Note the welded steel fuselage framing; in contrast to British planes, this was a very different approach to construction. (Fokker Team Schorndorf)

The Burbridge Committee[81] highlighted gross inefficiencies in British aircraft companies as a whole—this took the heat off the RAF as it was stated that they weren't the only ones that were to blame. O'Gorman and Henderson were tireless in their efforts to explain to the public that half of what they did was problem-solving and finding remedies for poor aspects of designs produced in the private sector.[82] In contrast, the private sector were the ones who were largely producing excellent designs such as Bristol and Sopwith, so apologies like this didn't really ring true. In addition to problems in management research and development, there was also logistical problems in supplying materials; from fittings, engines and their components, wood, linen, dope, etc.[83]

The S.E. series

The S.E.1 was not really part of the design path that would lead to the S.E.5. It had a short and unhappy career—looking more like an awkward variation of a Wright or Farman pusher. It was designed by de Havilland in 1912, and was obviously a nod to what had worked in the past (pusher biplane, with twin rudders and canard elevator) rather than looking toward the future.

In January 1912, O'Gorman sent out a list of new types of aircraft—including a small, light, fast scout designed by de Havilland—it was called the B.S.1. However, before it made its first flight in March of that year it was renamed the S.E.2 (initials now meant "Scouting Experimental").[84] The S.E.2 was as beautiful and modern as the S.E.1 was ugly and awkward. It had a streamlined cowling and fuselage, nicely rounded wingtips, a single bay cellule structure (reminiscent of the N-28). It could do 92 mph in level flight and could climb 800 feet/minute. Rudder authority was found lacking however, so a larger rudder was fitted in late March. De Havilland took her up and lost control suffering a non-fatal crash; this marked the end of his time at The Royal Aircraft Factory.

At this point, Henry P. Folland was given the project following de Havilland's departure. Folland came from humble beginnings; working his way up in engineering through various auto companies including Daimler—where he fell in love with airplanes—coming to the RAF in 1912.[85] Folland rebuilt the remnants of the wrecked S.E.2 during the summer of 1912 using a smaller 80 hp Gnome with an enlarged tail section. This proved to be a good "hack" and was appropriated by the War Office and sent to 5 Squadron in January 1914 for three months. It was rigorously used and evaluated, finally being rebuilt yet again with a traditional rear fuselage

S.E.2, the rebuilt B.S.1. using an 80 hp Gnome.

S.E.2 serial 609. 80 hp Gnome.

S.E.2a.

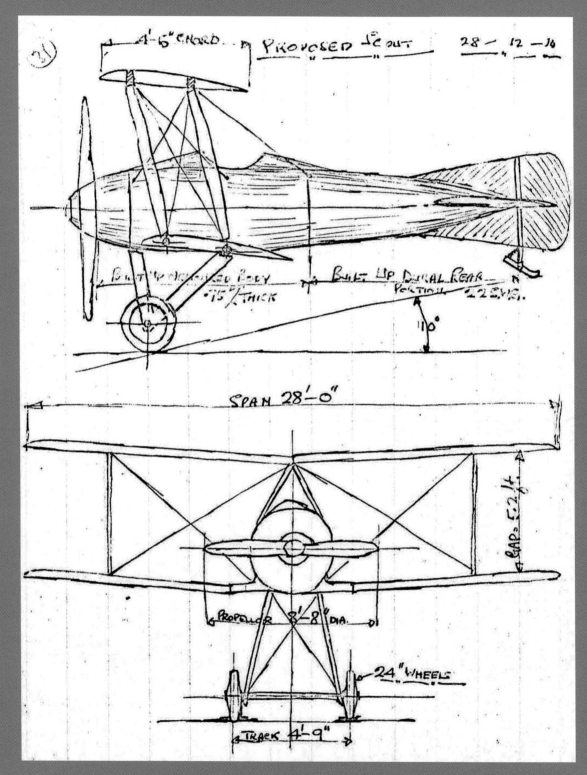

Folland's sketch of the S.E.2. (Farnborough Air Sciences Trust—all Folland notebook references come from FAST)

S.E.4a with 80 HP Le Rhone engine. (Greg VanWyngarden)

(stringers and linen) in place of the monocoque construction.[86] In addition, the cowling was given a sharper entry and a spinner on the prop to make the nose more streamlined. It also featured the new "RAF wires" which were streamlined rigging wires produced at the RAF. In this configuration it was sent to France in October 1914 until March 1915, when it was withdrawn.[87]

It must have been frustrating for design teams all over England to adhere to the War Office's mandate of no fighter exceeding 100 mph top speed. This in effect meant that no fast fighters could be developed—made even more infuriating due to the lack of this restriction in other countries—like Germany and France.

An S.E.3 was stillborn; not making it to the full-sized templating phase due to shortages of the new Gnome Lambda-Lambda—a double-banked rotary that boasted 160 hp, the object of which was to build the fastest plane in the world, in flagrant disregard for the War Office's mandate! Folland relished this new-found freedom and set out developing the S.E.4 which featured extensive streamlining around the engine—on par with Spads and Albatros fighters, single struts between the wings, flaperons, ply-skinned fuselage (like Germans) lightweight Ramie fabric replaced Irish linen, and all control horns and turnbuckles were internal.[88] On July 27, 1914, a speed of 134 mph and rate of climb of 1,600 feet/min. was recorded. It was commandeered for military service but crashed before it could be deployed. Finally, three S.E.4as were built in 1915 which had re-designed slab-sided fuselages, and 80 hp Gnome engines. These saw service with the home defense, but were not deemed frontline aircraft due to the rapidly changing context and criteria for a successful fighter—now aircraft needed to be efficient pursuit planes; not the passive scouts or reconnaissance planes that characterized the first six months after the outbreak.

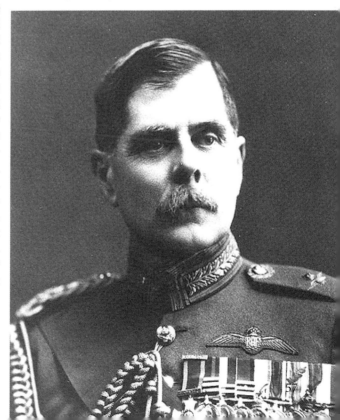

Major-General Hugh Trenchard, who issued a new set of criteria in February 1916 that would allow development of the S.E.5, Camel, and F.2B.

S.E.4 with V-undercarriage, later serialled 628 and featured a 160 hp Gnome.

In Profile
RAF S.E.5a

RAF S.E.5a: (5687) No. 60 Squadron,
RAF; Baisieux, France; November 1917.

ronnybarprofiles@gmail.com

The S.E.5

Due to the slaughter of British pilots flying the outdated B.E.2s during the "Fokker Scourge," and under mounting public outcry, and—by extension—government pressure to resolve this problem, Trenchard generated a new set of criteria for a new scout/fighter that he imposed upon the aircraft manufacturers in February 1916:

- Climb to 10,000 feet in 15 minutes
- Do at least 100 mph at 10,000 feet
- Ceiling of no less than 18,000 feet
- Having an endurance of 3–4 hrs.
- Be able to fire straight ahead

These new parameters for a successful fighter led to the development of the Camel, Bristol F.2b fighter, and the S.E.5.[89] In France, Louis Béchereau had developed the awkward and unsuccessful A.2 which utilized the Hispano-Suiza engine, the silver lining to that cloud being the eventual genesis of the Spad VII.

In August 1915, the British War Office brokered a deal whereby England would supply raw materials in exchange for the French supplying 150 Le Rhône and 50 of the new Hispano-Suiza engines, with Wolseley being licensed to build same in their factory in Birmingham.[90]

Also in August, the first Hispano-Suiza ("Hisso") arrived at the Royal Aircraft Factory—and with a seeming lack of imagination they built a pulpit fighter just like the French A.2! It was built from a B.E.2 and it was called the B.E.9; author Nick Garton commented that it "lived for a mercifully brief period and inflicted no undue casualties."[91] Both Trenchard and Dowding were underwhelmed by the aircraft.

The incandescent successes of French ace Georges Guynemer could not be seen as a fluke, in that an increasing number of French pilots were also successful in the new Spad VIIs. It became plainly apparent

A Spad VII B9913 painted in RFC colors.

Georges Guynemer, by "Lucien" (unknown painter) in the Musée de la Légion d'Honneur et des Ordres de Chevalerie, Paris.

to British leadership that the Hisso-powered fighter was a significant portion of meeting Trenchard's requirement for a fast, high-flying aircraft with forward-firing machine gun.[92]

At this juncture, the Admiralty, no doubt spurred on by an enthusiastic and prescient Winston Churchill, pushed for an order of 8,000 Hissos to be built in Britain. The cost and finished engines would be shared between Britain, France, and Russia—numbers were 3500, 3000, and 1500 respectively.[93] To attain this goal, Wolseley's factory in Birmingham would be supported by the French manufacturer Emile Mayen—and so the Admiralty's plan was operationalized.

However, the real problem was that there was no (British) design worthy of the new engine. Presumably these engines would be for British-built Spads like those built by Mann Egerton—or for replacements for French-built Spads equipping British squadrons. Thus, the Admiralty ordered enough Spads VIIs from France to equip two squadrons.[94]

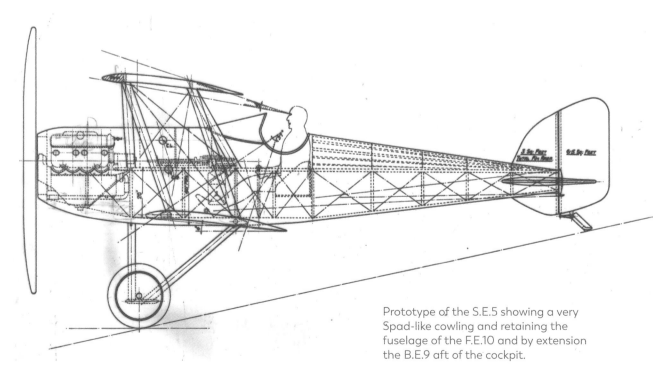

Prototype of the S.E.5 showing a very Spad-like cowling and retaining the fuselage of the F.E.10 and by extension the B.E.9 aft of the cockpit.

Meanwhile, the Bristol F.2 was under development, Sopwith was finalizing plans for the F.1 Camel, and the RAF was ostensibly working on a scout prototype that would leverage the Hispano-Suiza to advantage. Sefton Brancker was sent to the RAF to see how they were making out. Doubtless he was horrified to see the F.E.10, a single-seat pulpit fighter. Noting instantly the similarity to the ill-fated B.E.9, he insisted on a tractor like the Spad. A sketch was distributed by Frank Gooden—it looked much closer to a Spad at which point Folland began drawing up plans—this was the genesis of the S.E.5. Interestingly, the tail aft of the cockpit of the F.E.10 survived and became that of the S.E.5.

Seemingly, Folland took significant inspiration from the line of S.E. fighters after de Havilland's departure, and was supported by John Kenworthy, Chief Draughtsman. These three were overseen by Chief Engineer Frederick Green and Stanley Hiscocks as Chief Draughtsman—both of whom reported to O'Gorman.[95] Both Folland and Kenworthy also relied on input from Major Frank W. Gooden.

One of the more advanced features of the development of the new fighter was Folland's reliance upon testing using the wind tunnel at Farnborough—especially with regards to cowlings for the Hisso. In addition, tests were done on fairings at wing roots but the gain in performance vs. the production cost was not practical. The new design called for upper and lower planes of equal span (forward stagger of 4°) using the standard RAF15 pattern airfoil, rigged in a single bay using the RAF wires.[96] Looking at the drawing of the prototype, the forward cowling looks very much like a Spad VII, which is not surprising given the success of that fighter.

The upper wing would carry a reserve fuel tank—plans originally called for main tank to be in the leading edge but this was cost prohibitive, and the wings were fixed at 5° degrees of dihedral and the stagger angle was also increased to the same.[97]

The wing layout was driven by the combat experience of tail chasing in a steep bank, and if the plane could remain stable in such maneuvers than all the better—added bonus, the plane would return to straight and level based on amount of dihedral, so if pilot was wounded, blinded, incapacitated, etc. he would stand a fighting chance of surviving.[98]

The fuselage was built using standard wire-braced/box-girder construction, much in the fashion outlined in Chapter Two, using jigs to fabricate and assemble the spruce timbers. The engine was supported by bearers made from ash that were in turn supported by bulkheads made of spruce reinforced ply, culminating with the firewall which separated the engine area from the rest of the plane. The longerons and struts were secured with mild steel stamped fittings to which piano wire and turnbuckles hardened the entire structure.[99] Buttressing the firewall and baffle plate was the 28-gallon fuel tank which rested/was bolted directly on the upper longerons in front of the cockpit, with the tank itself forming the turtle deck for that portion. Plywood was used for the remaining turtle deck around the cockpit. Originally there was going to be a machine gun firing through the hub of prop using a geared Hisso, but these were in short supply and prone to failure, so this was abandoned in favor of single Vickers machine gun let into a trough in the fuel tank.[100] The Vickers gun would use the new Constantinesco interrupter gear, which relied on a hydraulic system through which pulses were transmitted to interrupt firing between prop blades. The mounting for the Vickers gun was a steel tripod that was also mounted to the upper longerons.

An interesting feature of the ply turtle deck on the starboard side was a small plex-covered aperture which allowed natural light into the cockpit to provide easier viewing of the instruments. To port was another panel to allow access to the Vickers gun. The cockpit had a ply floor that mounted atop the lower longerons, and a ply apron (similar to Spad) upon which the clock, altimeter, and magneto switches were mounted. The main instrument panel featured the transfer air selector valve, fuel air pressure gauge, fuel selector switch, airspeed, accelerometer, tachometer, and temperature and pressure gauges.[101]

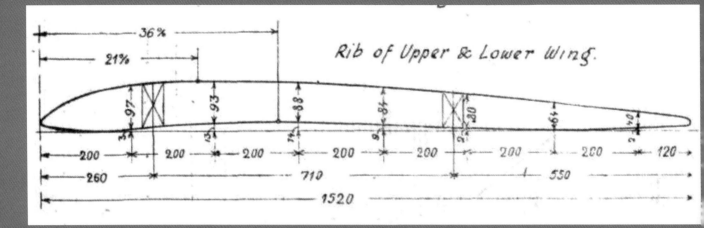

RAF15 pattern airfoil. (*Flight*, May 9, 1918)

Showing stylized fuselage framing. From "The English S.E.V.A. Single Seat Fighter." Translated from contemporary German report in *Deutsche Luftfahrer Zeitschrift* for *Flight*, May 9, 1918.

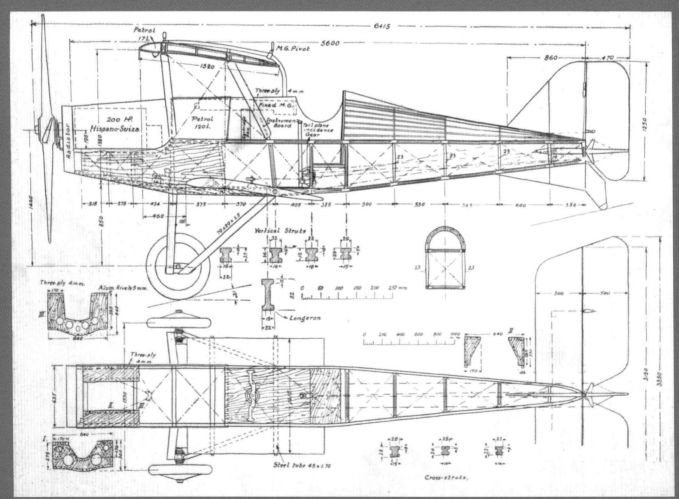

Fuselage framing of a replica S.E.5a built by John Saunders. Note the interplay of spruce, plywood, and metal fittings, working together to form a very strong, and straightforward structure. Note also the lightening grooves carved into the various struts and cross-pieces. The cambered pieces will form the foundation for the fuel tank. The black tube steel pieces protruding from the wing root will serve as attachment points for the lower wing panels. (John Saunders)

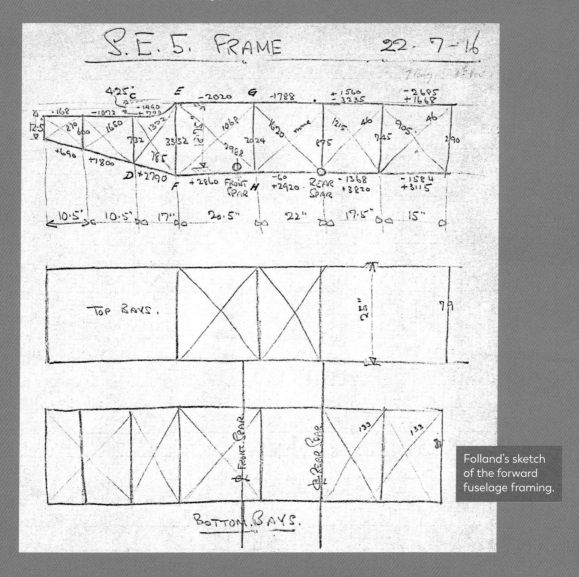

Folland's sketch of the forward fuselage framing.

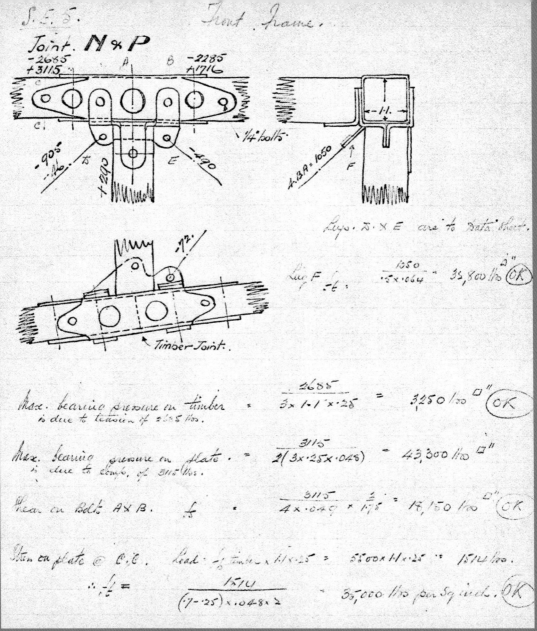

S.5.5.   Front. frame.

Joint. N & P
-2685
+3115

A   B -2285
      +1716

C

C1

-90°

+290

-490

E

¼" bolts

4.BA + 1050

F

← 1.1 →

-72

Timber Joint.

Lugs. D. & E are to Data sheet.

Lug F -6 : $\dfrac{1050}{.5 \times .064}$ = 35,800 lbs ◻" (OK)

Max. bearing pressure on timber = $\dfrac{2685}{3 \times 1.1 \times .25}$ = 3,250 lbs ◻" (OK)
is due to tension of 2685 lbs.

Max. bearing pressure on plate = $\dfrac{3115}{2(3 \times .25 \times .048)}$ = 43,300 lbs ◻"
is due to comp. of 3115 lbs.

Shear on Bolts A & B. f_s = $\dfrac{3115}{4 \times .049 \times 1.75}$ = 19,150 lbs ◻" (OK)

Stress on plate @ C.L.   Load: f_s timber × 1.1 × .25 = 5500 × 1.1 × .25 = 1514 lbs.

∴ f_s = $\dfrac{1514}{(.7-.25) \times .048 \times 2}$ = 35,000 lbs per sq inch. (OK)

Above, Folland's sketch for the fitting surrounding the engine mounting framing. I believe this illustrates the fitting that joined two pieces of timber.

Exposed engine bed framing showing the variety of metal fittings, plywood, and solid stock that comprised the structure.

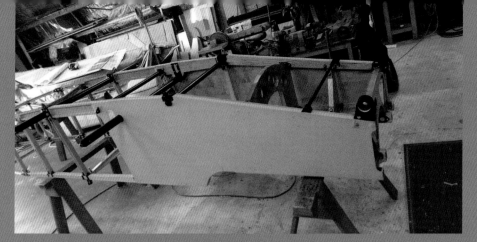

John Saunders' replica S.E.5a fuselage inverted showing the steel cross pieces more clearly, which form attachment points for wings as well as landing gear struts. Note also the composite engine formers that are made from spruce solid stock and plywood. (John Saunders)

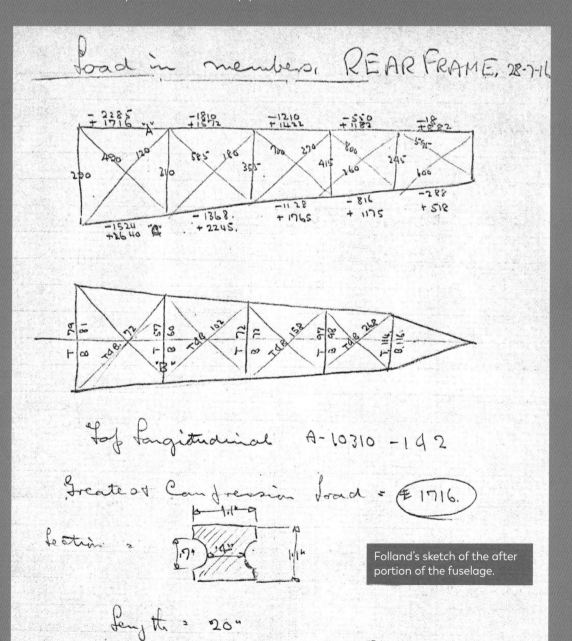

Folland's sketch of the after portion of the fuselage.

John Saunders' replica S.E.5a fuselage displaying a wealth of information. Note the fuel tank that has baffles integrated into the interior structure to prevent fuel from sloshing wildly which could affect stability. Also visible is the notch out to accept the Vickers machine gun. The stub wing roots have been built encasing the steel tubes which will anchor the lower wing panels. (John Saunders)

The S.E.5 had a remarkably comfortable cockpit for the time. It was roomy and deep, with particular attention paid to ergonomics for ease and comfort of the pilot. As with many British aircraft of the time, it had fairly complete instrumentation. However, the cockpit took a bit of work—the first seat was needlessly complicated; it adjusted vertically and fore and aft and was armor plated. It was replaced by a simple wicker seat mounted on a piece of plywood. Like most WWI aircraft, the fabric covering the panels were laced to allow removal for inspection of the underlying airframe.

Initially, the undercarriage was made from streamlined steel tube, with the axle in a streamline fairing and set up on bungees.[102] The upper wing center section also attached using steel tube that was encased in wood fairings, then wrapped with linen tape; inside these fairings piping was led down from the gravity tank to the engine. The linen tape could be removed and the fairings disassembled to allow access to tubing—both structural and for fuel.[103] The rudder post and tail skid were quite an interesting piece of engineering as the skid was steerable, and

Folland's sketch of the fittings for the intersection of the forward cabane, and firewall area of the fuselage framing.

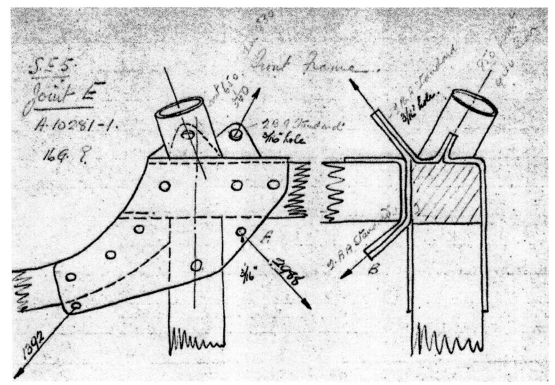

John Saunders: Building a S.E.5a

When asked why he does what he does, John Saunders stated that "old aircraft are sort of in my blood." His father flew Harvards & Tigermoths in the Royal New Zealand Air Force in the 1950s, and his grandfather on wife's side trained on French Caudrons during WWI. John noted that he had always been passionate about aircraft for as long as he can remember. He trained initially in the Royal New Zealand Air Force—but the WWI bug was probably inspired by an old movie—or Biggles books!

John has an A&P/ IA , and Mechanical Engineering Degree, but notes that for this sort of work—hand skills & patience are paramount. He's a real purist when it comes to WWI aircraft, disliking scaled, modern engined "improved" WWI look-a-likes! To do it "right" he states you need to start with the correct engine, original drawings, and go from there. He notes that too many people start building fuselages, then end up simplify them, and then have to compromise on an engine such that the result is a big expensive "homebuilt"—instead of an authentic copy of an aircraft.

John is building an S.E.5a from drawings for the S.E.5a from original Royal Aircraft Establishment drawings held at the Public Records Office at Kew, London as well as some lovely assembly drawings done by Jim Kiger from Replicraft out of CA. He had this to say about the S.E.5a:

The quirkiest thing about the S.E.5a is that it is so "government designed"—way over-designed compared to, say, a Sopwith Camel (private company run by Tommy Sopwith) so all joints are glued, screwed or bolted into fittings, and then braced with wires … I'm guessing they didn't believe in glue … so really, really strong. It is a very complicated aircraft—more like, say, a 1930s Great Lakes Sport Biplane … than something which flew 13–14 years after Orville & Wilbur.

Building an S.E.5a is a long-term deal … takes years to build contacts, find parts, get drawings etc etc. I started out when my Kansas City friend, Fred Barber, convinced me that a WWI aircraft is very possible to build and fly … but you have to start with the correct WWI engine … so if I found a Hisso, I should build an S.E.5a, if I found a Le Rhône … build a Camel … wise advice as I'm interested in building one as close as possible to the original … and, sadly, find no great interest in scaled, or re-engined aircraft … but for a real WWI machine, I'd travel half way around the world.

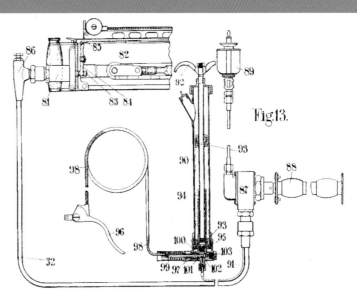

Illustration depicting the Constantinesco-Colley interrupter gear that relied upon wave pulses transmitted through fluid to stop the machine gun from firing when the blade was in line with the field of fire.

Above, various instruments and components for John Saunders' S.E.5a instrument panel. Finding period instruments for a replica aircraft can sometimes take years. (John Saunders)

The cockpit of the S.E.5a. Note the plywood apron surrounding the cockpit and forming a basis for some instruments. This panel also served to stiffen/strengthen the cockpit. (Image courtesy of Darren Harbar)

the horizontal stabilizer featured adjustable incidence that was actuated on the rudder post. The trim mechanism was elegant—using cable and a chain that operated a screw mechanism that adjusted the entire tail plane at its rear attachment point pivoting at the leading edge. The rear brace wires traveled up and down with the rear spar of the horizontal stabilizer which featured large elevators of 15.8 sq. feet (combined).[104] The vertical fin was formed from streamlined steel tubing over which linen was stretched, as was the rudder. Folland computed in one of his notebooks that the rudder was 6 sq. feet, with a loading of 20 lbs. per sq. foot. (see page 70.)

All four wing panels were made in identical fashion and were of identical plan form. The main spars were spruce to which ply formers were slid over and secured (spacing was different on upper and lower wings) nose ribs were used to improve the airfoil's entry and retain the shape. Wing bracing (especially the flying wires) was extensive using streamlined RAF wire.[105] Folland's notebooks contain extensive attention to detail with regards to the metal fittings and arrangement for the rigging—as these crucial bits of metal supported all the wooden components under the stresses of combat and as such required careful consideration and design; they needed to be just strong enough with a margin for overload, and simultaneously had to be as light as possible.

The most problematic aspect of the new fighter was the empennage—Folland wanted an adjustable trim mechanism inside the cockpit, and a steerable tail skid tied to the rudder bar. Completed drawings and specs were submitted to War Office in August 1916—they responded with an order for three prototypes: A4561, 62, and 63. In addition, a pre-production run of 24 airframes were also ordered. The engine would be the Hispano-Suiza 8Aa 150 hp direct-drive. The third prototype, A4563, would become the prototype S.E.5a powered by the 200 hp Hispano-Suiza.

The first three S.E.5 prototypes were built (A4561–63) during ten weeks in the summer of 1916. Between November 1916 and April 1917 the definitive specification for the S.E.5a was attained through trial and error, loss of Gooden (see page 77), 56 Squadron's experimentation, and the preferences of Capt. Albert Ball. The

The wooden struts comprising John Saunders' replica S.E.5a landing gear. Note the laminated steel fittings that bind the struts together at their apex, and the elongated holes which allow the axles to rebound and act as a shock absorber. (John Saunders)

The landing gear of the S.E.5a after the steel tube struts had been replaced by wooden legs. Note that the bungee area is enclosed with a bulbous fairing.

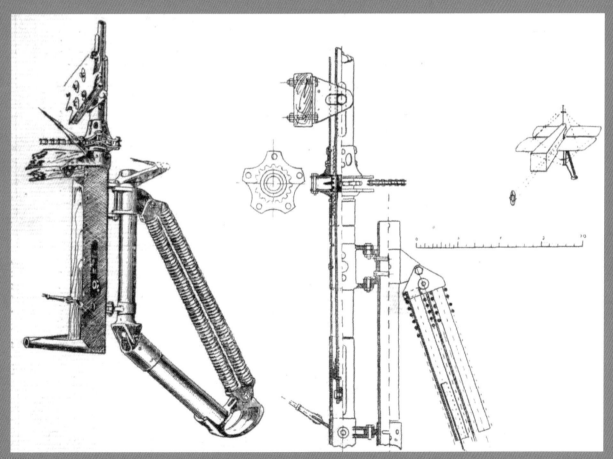

The steerable and shock-absorbing tail skid of the S.E.5a. Note the horn atop the vertical post to which control cables were attached. Also note the chain drive mechanism which operated the variable incidence of the horizontal stabilizer. From "The English S.E.V.A. Single Seat Fighter." Translated from contemporary German report in *Deutsche Luftfahrer Zeitschrift* for *Flight*, May 9, 1918.

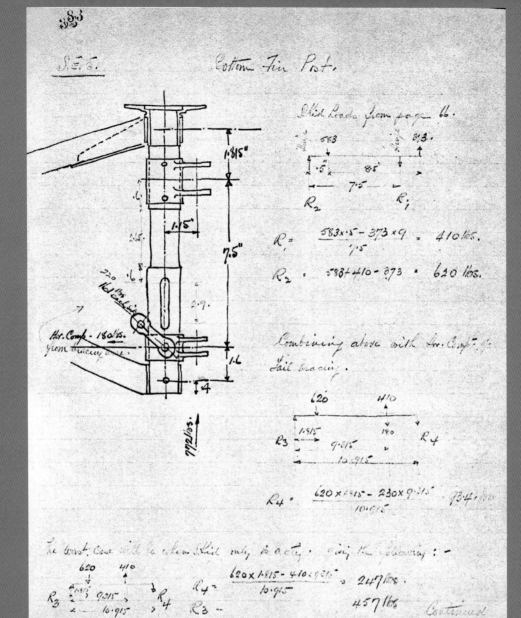

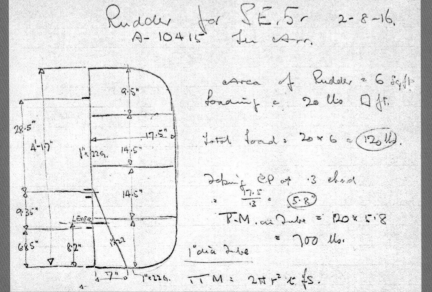

Above, sketch of the rudder post for the S.E.5 H. P. Folland notebooks (four in total), while serving at the Royal Aircraft Factory from 1912–1916.

Folland's drawing of the rudder area for S.E.5.

S.E.5a with a shortened wingspan, smaller windscreen, and an internally mounted gravity tank in the upper wing center section began arriving at the front in May 1917, with Capt. Albert Ball flying the first example: A8898.[106]

Gooden had a clear head and sense about airplanes that few had in 1916. He had this to say about the S.E.5: "She's a pixie."[107] British Ace Capt. Albert Ball was a different story. He was used to his Nieuports which he loved due to their nimble handling; the biggest problem with the S.E.5 in his mind was that it wasn't a Nieuport and had a different set of strengths and weaknesses that couldn't be absorbed in an instant. Ball disliked the S.E and lobbied against it; his experience with Royal Aircraft Factory planes was not good. He had flown the B.E.2 and hated it, and he was involved deeply in a rival project that was meant to utilize the new Hisso engine. Both Albert and his father were shareholders in Austin Motor Co. Ltd.—and they were developing what they hoped was a world-class fighter.[108] When Ball test flew the S.E.5 he already had approval from General David Henderson to proceed with his Austin fighter, so possibly he was not approaching the S.E with an unbiased opinion. It is difficult to know what proportion of his dissatisfaction with the new fighter was due to his own financial gain, his love of Nieuports, or distrust of aircraft produced by the RAF. In any event, these factors coalesced to form an initial negative opinion of the fighter in his mind.

That being said, Ball likely realized that he and his squadron mates would inevitably have to fly the new plane, and so he did offer some suggested improvements to the Scout. They included a fairing headrest for the pilot and a Lewis gun mounted on the top plane—no doubt a carry-over from his time spent in Nieuports. Fitting this gun required re-designing of the center section; strengthening the structure to absorb the shock from the gun recoil. Ball also recommended losing the "greenhouse" canopy structure in favor of a simple Triplex glass single pane windscreen—the argument being it obstructed visibility and if shattered, the pilot would suffer grievous injuries. He also advocated for longer exhaust stacks—keeping engine exhaust out of the pilot's face and directed aft of the cockpit area (just like the Spads).

Prototype A4561 had an engine-driven air pump, whereas the A4562 had a wind-driven unit mounted beneath the cockpit. On Christmas Eve 1916, Frederick Selous flew with Frank Gooden, each flying one of the two prototypes. Selous had this to say:

The wing panels for John Saunders' replica S.E.5a. Note the compression ribs as well as the standard rib webs. Riblets were fitted from the leading edge to the first spar to preserve the entry of the airfoil thus increasing efficiency of same. (Image courtesy of John Saunders)

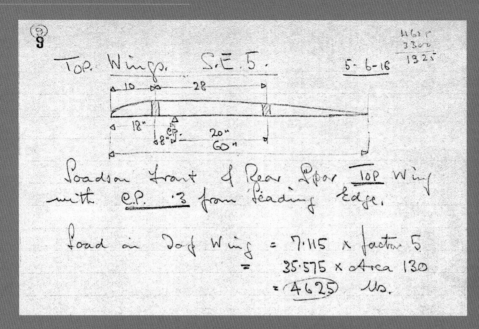

Folland's sketch of the upper wing airfoil and spar spacing for the S.E.5. Also noted is the "center of pressure" with is indicated as being 18 inches from the leading edge.

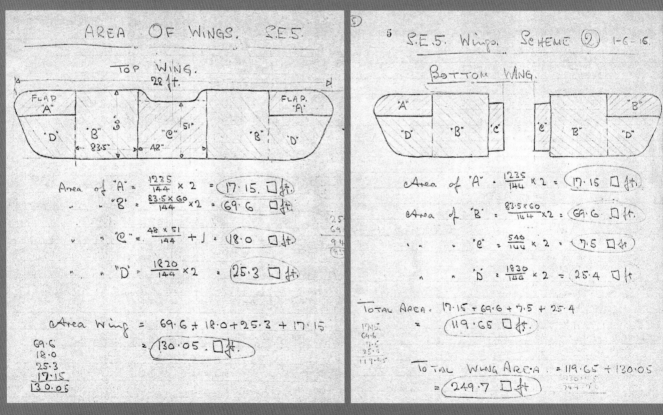

Folland's sketch of the S.E.5 upper wings showing area calculations.

Bottom wings plan view for the S.E.5 showing wing area calculations.

S.E.5 A4561 first prototype. Note the external gravity tank on the upper wing.

Control elevator: the S.E.5 is slightly lighter in the elevator than the Spad VII but the machine is harder to keep in a steep dive. Laterally: there is not any difference between the S.E.5 and the Spad VII. View: the view in all directions is very good [S.E], much better than the Spad, especially forwards and downwards. Climb and Speed: this cannot be judged accurately without flying the machines together, but the S.E.5 has a much greater range of speed than the Spad and will fly at 45 mph [unlike the Spad]. General flying: although the S.E.5 is stable it can be maneuvered quite as well as the Spad. The S.E.5 can be landed slower than the Spad and has a much flatter glide.[109]

Roderic Hill came from Ball's former squadron and unlike Ball, Hill liked the S.E:

The S.E.5 has, in my opinion, certain advantages over the Nieuport and Spad: its speed is good; it lands as slowly as the Nieuport and more slowly than the Spad; it is stronger than the Spad; its gun mounting is superior. It's disadvantage with respect to the Nieuport is that it cannot be maneuvered with quite the same rapidity, although at high altitudes, maneuvers should be possible with a much smaller loss of height.[110]

S.E.5 A8904 front view. Note the steel tube landing gear struts, green house windscreen, and unique shape of the radiator. (Photo courtesy of Greg VanWyngarden)

Capt. Albert Ball in an S.E.5 of 56 Squadron, London Colney, 1917. (Photo courtesy of Greg VanWyngarden)

Ball in the cockpit of an S.E.5, April 1917, that has had its "greenhouse" windscreen removed and replaced with a single pane Triplex glass windscreen. (Photo courtesy of Greg VanWyngarden)

An early S.E.5a—the tube steel landing gear still in use. S.E.5a B539 84 Squadron Beauchamp Proctor. (Photo courtesy of Greg VanWyngarden)

S.E.5a F904 (G-EBIA) of The Shuttleworth Collection showing the modified wooden landing gear that became standard on production planes.

S.E.5a F8953 85 Squadron.

A S.E.5a D3540
replica flying
among the clouds.

James McCudden's 56 Squadron S.E.5a B4891. McCudden was an outstanding British "Ace" fighter pilot.

As a result of Selous and Hill's feedback, a number of layout modifications were incorporated into the S.E.5's cockpit—e.g. the tailplane trim wheel gained a knob for ease of use with gloved hands at altitude, the gun-trigger levers were adjustable to where the pilot preferred, and an extended loading handle was fitted to the Vickers, the release lever for Lewis was repositioned and storage for extra Lewis magazines was built into the dash. An engine decelerator was also installed for emergencies.[111]

The revised A4562 was flown by Gooden on January 28, 1917, and while doing mild aerobatics near Farnborough, the port wing cell collapsed at 1,500 feet after he pulled out of a loop. Gooden perished in the resulting crash.[112] An immediate investigation was launched and it was discovered that the wing spars were close to breaking on all the prototypes and this is what happened on the fatal crash; the compression ribs had carried too much vertical flex which was transferred to the spar, weakening it over time. The solution to the weakness was simple: plywood webbing that reinforced these ribs solved the problem. Upon further testing, the spars were seen to break at 5.5gs which was unacceptable such that the spars were thickened. Moreover, the span outboard of the interplanes was under the most strain such that the wings were shortened from 28 to

James McCudden in the cockpit of his S.E.5a. (Photo courtesy of Greg VanWyngarden)

26 feet 7 inches and squaring the previously tapered wingtips—these modifications pushed the S.E.5 into the S.E.5a designation.[113]

Mass production began with contract airframes from Martinsyde and Vickers which were delivered to 56 Squadron in July 1917. 56 Squadron requested that the undercarriage be made stronger; so the steel tube struts were replaced by rosewood of more robust proportions. This became standard for all new factory airframes and operational aircraft would be retro-fitted, however, due to the difficulty in getting rosewood, cypress was used instead (it was probably also much lighter).[114]

In spite of all the calculations, intentions, careful design and testing, the crucible of combat was and is unique and is really the only way to adequately evaluate a given aircraft's design, construction, and suitability for a given task. Early in 1918, S.E.5as began experiencing wing failures during and after diving. Bill Lambert, author of *Combat Report* (London: William Kimber, 1973), had this happen to his S.E.5a:

> I heard a sharp crack like a shot from a Vicker's gun; the aeroplane lurched a little and I felt a quiver through the fuselage and into the seat of my pants. I noticed what appeared to be slight flutter in my top wings and looking through the center section I noticed one of the cross bracing wires had broken.[115]

The problem stemmed from the area outboard of the interplane struts, where the wings had the least support. The solution was to strengthen the framing around the ailerons, after which wing failures tapered off dramatically.

In terms of the appearance of the S.E.5a as seen at the front, the paint color for the S.E.5a was PC10 or "khaki green" or the reddish brown color PC12 which was used in particular for the Middle Eastern squadrons, with the undersides of wings and tail treated with clear varnish over dope.[116] Although fairly dull in appearance when contrasted with Germany's Flying Circus or some of the French paint schemes, 56 Squadron displayed the greatest variety of markings on their S.E.5as.[117]

Major Edward "Mick" Mannock—an advocate of putting the good of the many over personal achievement. (Photo courtesy of Greg VanWyngarden)

Replica Airco D.H.5 A9242 (ZK-JOQ) taxiing in preparation for takeoff. It is in the markings of an Australian Flying Corps aircraft with "New South Wales No.14 Women's Battleplane" on its side.

Aircraft Manufacturing Company (Airco)

In 1912, the Aircraft Manufacturing Company (AMC, later known as Airco) was created by industrialist George Holt Thomas, and was located in Hendon. Thomas was an advocate for British aviation development—he also kept tabs on French innovations—especially Farman, and was at the meet in 1909 at Rheims. He organized the British aviation meeting at Blackpool, and arranged demonstration flights around London.[118] He became manager of French aviator Louis Paulhan who, in 1910, won a £10,000 prize for flying from London to Manchester.[119] After seeing French use of the airplane for reconnaissance and artillery spotting, he wrote to the *Daily Mail* on September 17, 1910 stating, "A new weapon of the utmost importance in war has appeared, and with that weapon our army is wholly unprovided."[120] By the outbreak of the war, aviator William Taylor Birchenough worked as a test pilot for the company, and Holt Thomas learned that Geoffrey de Havilland was fed up with his employment at the Royal Aircraft Factory as it was overly bureaucratic with no real opportunity to design aircraft. Holt Thomas offered de Havilland that which he craved: to be chief designer at his company. De Havilland would play a seminal role during WWI with Airco and provided signature aircraft that would become synonymous with the company. De Havilland's designs could be recognized at a glance by the D.H. that preceded the number of a particular design (e.g. D.H.2). As de Havilland was at the center of this company, it is worth describing his evolution in greater detail.

A portrait of Sir Geoffrey de Havilland by Sir Oswald Birley, 1940.

Geoffrey de Havilland was born on July 27, 1882. His father was a preacher and had his own parish in Nuneaton, Warwickshire, where Geoffrey spent most of his childhood, and it was here that his two sisters and brother were born as well.

Both Geoffrey and his brother Ivon showed an early aptitude and interest in mechanical devices, and although his father wanted him to enter the clergy, he began training in 1900 at the Crystal Palace Engineering School, culminating with him and his brother building their own car and motorcycle. After three years he moved to an apprenticeship at Willans & Robinson of Rugby, Warwickshire where he built a better motorcycle. In 1905, he became a draughtmsman at the Wolseley Tool & Motor Car Co. in Birmingham. Within the year, boredom set in and he left, taking a job designing buses for the Motor Omnibus Construction Co. at Walthamstow, but this too would not hold Geoffrey's interest.

In Profile
AMC D.H.2

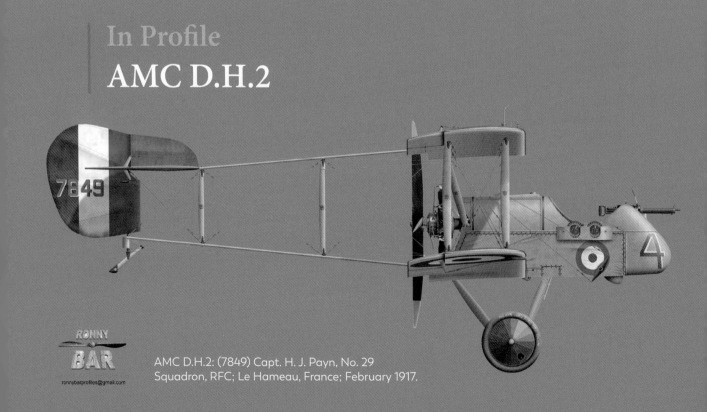

AMC D.H.2: (7849) Capt. H. J. Payn, No. 29 Squadron, RFC; Le Hameau, France; February 1917.

RONNY BAR
ronnybarprofiles@gmail.com

When Wilbur Wright awed the continent with his command of his aircraft at Le Mans in 1908, Geoffrey decided on the spot that his future lay in aviation. He borrowed £1000 from his grandfather and began to design his own airplane, got married, and his new bride was put to work on his plane—some honeymoon! Although the first effort was unsuccessful—stalling on takeoff, followed by a wing collapse—his second flew in the spring of 1910 and it was good enough to be purchased by the Royal Balloon Factory at Farnborough. It was built by himself and Frank T. Hearle, and was an amalgam of various designs—the Farman influence was pronounced. He was paid £400 and it was called not surprisingly the Farman Experimental 1 or F.E.1.[121] It had a wingspan of 33.5 feet, spaced 5.5 feet apart between planes which were made from a double lamination of pegamoid, which was calico treated with celluloid.[122] At the tips were hinged winglets (aka ailerons) which controlled roll. There were elevators fitted forward and aft, spaced about 12 feet from the planes in either direction. This aircraft featured a "handle" that actuated the elevators and winglets/ailerons, with the engine being controlled by the left hand and bar-operated rudder.[123] The 200 lb. engine was of de Havilland's own design, and could produce 50 hp at 1500 revolutions of the two-bladed mahogany prop.

Soon after in 1911, de Havilland was hired as Chief Aircraft Designer and pilot at the Royal Balloon Factory. The eventual genesis of the D.H.2 can be seen as the gradual outcome of the system of planes and booms that began with the Wrights and Farman and gradually became refined with others of this ilk such as the F.E.1. Another way to view it was the necessity of using pusher propulsion to allow the gun to fire forward without hitting the prop as no practicable interrupting gear had been developed by the Allies yet. Evolving concurrently was the evolution of the tractor biplane with streamlined fuselage that was begun by Blériot. It is questionable whether this type (booms and planes) would have made it this far if not for the notoriety of the very early pioneers such as the Wrights.

In 1912, the Balloon Factory was renamed the Royal Aircraft Factory and de Havilland joined the Special Reserve of the Royal Flying Corps (RFC). He worked at the Royal Aircraft Factory for three-and-a-half years working on the S.E.1, B.E.1, B.E.2, F.E.2, and the B.S.1 which was by far the most advanced tractor biplane of the time. It had a monocoque fuselage that faired cleanly into a full cowl, and featured single-bay planes with elegantly rounded tips, a full-flying rudder and a horizontal stabilizer and elevator that resembled the signature German Albatros fighters. A drawback was that this plane still featured the now outdated wing-warping. It could do 91.4 mph in level flight making it the fastest British aircraft of its day.[124] Seemingly, the monocoque approach to the S.E.1 inspired a redesign of the F.E.1—the F.E.2 which featured a streamlined nacelle in place of the awkward and dysfunctional canard elevator system. In 1914, he was made Chief Inspector of Airplanes, a job he hated as it wasn't design-related, which compelled him to leave the Royal Aircraft Factory in June 1914 to work for the Aircraft Manufacturing Company.

The first version of the F.E.2, 1911.

A later version of the F.E.2, 1913.

At the outbreak in 1914, de Havilland was called up but his injuries prevented him from serving at the front, so he was relegated to patrols off the east coast of Scotland. His country felt his talents were being wasted patrolling the Scottish coast so was summoned to resume his duties at the Aircraft Manufacturing Company. His first aircraft on the job was the D.H.1 which looked very similar to the F.E.2a series he designed at the RAF. Both of these aircraft were flown in January 1915. The fact that they were so similar raises questions as to the circumstances under which he left the RAF. In any event, the War Office went with the F.E.2b (production version of the F.E.2a) instead of the D.H.1, most likely due to the fact that the RAF was at that time receiving preferential attention from British leadership.[125]

In Profile
RAF F.E.2b

RONNY
BAR

ronnybarprofiles@gmail.com

RAF F.E.2b: (4290) 2Lt. E. Burton & 2Lt. F. W. Griffiths, No. 11 Squadron, RFC; Izel-le-Hameau, France; September 1916.

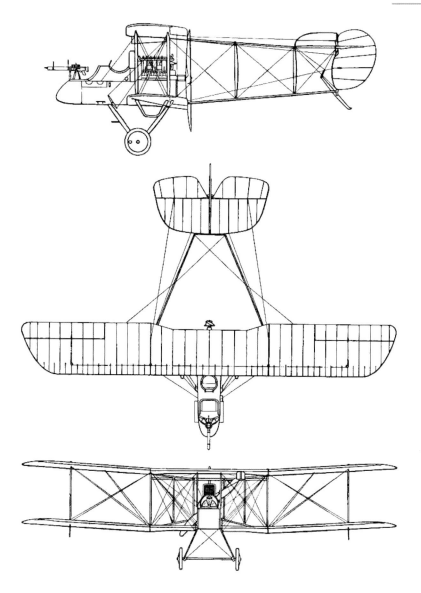

A three-view drawing of a D.H.1a.

J. M. Bruce commented that he felt de Havilland was likely unaware of Saulnier's gun synchronizing experiments; if he had been, the idea for the D.H.2 might have taken a very different design path—that of a tractor, like the S.E.2/S.B.1—instead of a pusher. Obviously, the chief advantage of pushers at this time was that there was no interference with the forward-firing gun's field of fire. The first prototype of the D.H.2 (#4732) flew in the summer of 1915, coinciding with the arrival of the Fokker Eindeckers at the Front. The D.H.2 had a 100 hp Monosoupape engine, metal booms with spruce vertical spars between the booms and planes. The nacelle was a combination of formed aluminum, traditional box-girder/wire-braced struts/ longerons, and some fabric. The fuel tank was gravity fed, and was mounted atop the upper plane—either centered or offset.

F.E.2a. Note the profusion of heavily rigged struts supporting the wings, this created a tremendous amount of drag coupled with engine of modest power made this aircraft an easy target.

Darren Harbar's image of a replica D.H.2 peeling off.

D.H.1. Note the nicely streamlined nacelle, and cleaner strut/rigging on the wings.

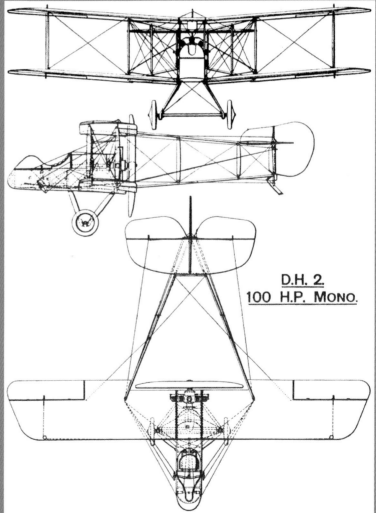

D.H. 2.
100 H.P. MONO.

A three-view drawing of the D.H.2, which featured a 100 hp Gnome Monosoupape engine.

D.H.2 seen without armament or pilot.

The single Lewis gun with its 47-round magazine was no match for the Eindeckers with their belt-fed Spandau machine guns that could fire over 200 rounds before needing to be re-armed. Lanoe Hawker stated that it was nearly impossible to fly the plane with one hand and aim a swiveling Lewis gun with the other. He tried to fix the gun to fire only forward, but this was overruled by leadership, arguing that the Nieuport 11 could swivel its gun upwards so therefore so too must the D.H.2.[126] It is true that eventually the D.H.2s featured a fixed, forward-firing setup for the gun, but it is unclear how this officially came to pass.

When the Albatros line of fighters made their beautiful but deadly debut over the Front in the fall of 1916, they rendered the nimble and draggy D.H.2 absolutely obsolete—one could argue that with the appearance of the Nieuport 11 they were obsolete even earlier. From mid-fall to March 1917, those flying the D.H.2s suffered grievously. The D.H.2s were officially replaced with Nieuport 17s in March 1917.[127] By May 1917, the D.H.5s began to appear for frontline duty and the D.H.2s were finally completely withdrawn by June.

D.H.2 painted in olive drab with a four-blade prop. Note absence of Lewis gun.

Reproduction of a D.H.2 in the permanent collection of the Omaka Aviation Heritage Centre.

Left, another view of Omaka's D.H.2. Note the fixed, forward-firing Lewis gun.

Below, the positioning of the Fokker Eindecker behind Omaka's D.H.2 tells the story, these two were bitter foes during the "Fokker Scourge."

The concept behind the D.H.5 was to have a clean tractor biplane with the good forward field of view of the pushers—not surprisingly as the D.H.2 had been successful in this regard. It had a backwards stagger of the wings to move the upper plane's leading edge aft of the pilot's head. The wings were of equal span of 25.75 feet with a chord of 4.5 feet, with dihedral on both wings of 172° and incidence of 2.5° on both wings except for the upper plane amidships which was only 2°.[128] The prototype emerged in late 1916 and was test flown at Hendon by Bentfield C. Hucks.[129] The wings featured unusually long ailerons that were hinged to the aft spars. Interestingly, rubber bungees provided the rebound for the ailerons initially (no return cables), but were later replaced by the standard cable and pulley system employed by Sopwith and the Royal Aircraft Factory.[130] The wing spars were spruce spindled out to form an "I" in section, and ribs were spaced between 9 ⅞ inches and 15 inches with two riblets between each rib.[131] Wings were fitted with anti-drag bracing and were considered very strong and well-made.

The basic fuselage structure was made in two parts that were butt-joined at the rear cabane struts. There was liberal use of 3 mm plywood for strength specifically under the horizontal stabilizer, and forward of the cockpit.[132] Ply is also used as the formers to give the fuselage its rounded sections. The forward portion had side bracing of large panels of ply with a latticework of lightening holes, and the tail bays of the rear portion were made similarly. At the core was the tried and true box-girder, wire-braced structure that served as the foundation for so many Allied aircraft. The horizontal stabilizer was fixed at 1° of incidence (and was not adjustable).[133]

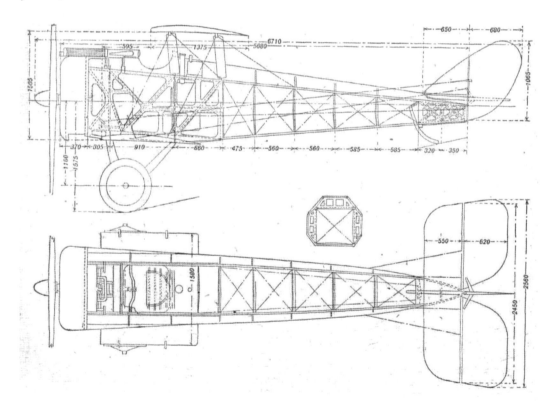

A line-drawing depicting the unique construction of the D.H.5 fuselage; it could be disassembled into two halves at the aft end of the rear cabane struts. (*Flight*, October 24, 1918)

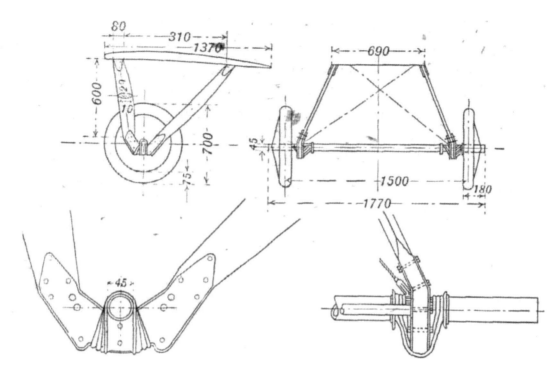

Undercarriage layout for the D.H.5.

The undercarriage was of solid spruce streamlined V-struts with a continuous (not split) axle that was free to rebound without any stops. The main fuel tank held 26.4 gallons of fuel, and oil tank held three gallons—both tanks were mounted behind the pilot, and there was an emergency gravity feed fuel tank holding 26 liters on the starboard upper plane.[134] The main fuel tank was pressurized by means of a small pump mounted to the port forward undercarriage strut. The instrument panel contained a tachometer, speedometer, altimeter, clock, magneto switch, and a compass—the D.H.5s built by Airco had an electrically lit panel for night flying.[135] To the left, fuel and oil throttles, and small hand pump for air. A single Vickers machine gun was fitted to fire through the prop using the Constantinesco interrupter gear, but it could also be elevated to about 60° to fire upwards in an effort to allow attacks from below while maintaining cruising speed.[136] Finally, it was powered by a 110 Le Rhône 9J rotary that was neatly cowled.

The D.H.5 was tested at the Central Flying School on December 9, 1916, and the flight report stated that the stability was good, as was pitch and roll, however the rudder had poor authority such that it was consequently redesigned to the shape that would survive all the way to the venerable Tiger Moth. The machine was easy to land and fly, and was handy and quick in the air.[137]

Performance at low altitudes was very good, and its speed of 100 mph at 10,000 feet was a distinct improvement over the D.H.2's 77 mph. However, the Sopwith Pup was able to do 104.5 mph with only a 80 hp engine, and could climb to 10,000 feet in 14 min. 25 sec., whereas the D.H.5 needed 16 min. 18 sec.; moreover, the Pup's ceiling was 17,500 feet vs. the D.H.5's 14,300 feet.[138] Bruce commented that since the Sopwith Pup could also beat the D.H.5's performance on all important metrics, it was curious that the D.H.5 was ordered in such quantity. It is possible that the government was trying to spread contracts around as far as possible to companies who showed promise. Airco had the successful D.H.2, so this would have garnered at least some support based

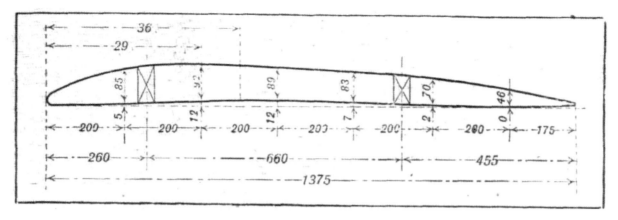

Airfoil for the D.H.5.

on a good track record. Still, the D.H.5 was also harder and more expensive to build than either of their Sopwith contemporaries, so perhaps augmenting an egalitarian stance, there were unseen politics at work.

Bruce also noted that the outstanding aspect of the D.H.5 was its structural strength. Oliver Stewart commented in Leonard Brigeman's *The Clouds Remember* (Aldershot: Gale & Poden Ltd. 1938) that it "could really dive." A D.H.5 was tested to destruction and bolts holding rigging fittings and controls broke before the wings did.[139] That being said, given the aforementioned superiority of comparable Sopwith aircraft, and with the Camel and S.E.5 nearing production and deployment, the D.H.5 didn't have much of a future at the Front.

De Havilland shifted gears and began designing two-seater reconnaissance/bomber aircraft such as the D.H.4 and eventually the D.H.9, so this concluded his role as a designer of fighters during WWI. De Havilland made a good amount of money on his designs so he could afford a nice home in Edgware where his third son John was born. However, late in the year the pressures of late war exigencies took their toll resulting in his collapse. He moved his family to Sussex where he hoped the quieter setting would ease his nerves, but the commute to work was too far, forcing him to live in Stanmore, Middlesex.[140]

A replica D.H.5 (N950JS)—the reserve gravity feed fuel tank on the upper wing and the reverse stagger of the wings are clearly visible.

A replica Avro 504 with tail up about to take off.

| A. V. Roe & Company (Avro)

Alliott Verdon Roe was the founder and driving force behind "Avro" Company—a name synthesized from his first two initials and the first two letters of his last name. A. V. Roe was characterized by impatience and a certain restlessness. He spoke with an "engaging eager quickness matching his enthusiastic but modest temperament."[141] His dad had given Roe a "Penny Farthing" bicycle in 1883 which fostered a lifelong affection for cycles. Roe had trained as a surveyor but found no work in England, so left Liverpool for Canada aboard the *Labrador* as a teen in 1892—only to find no work there either. He found humble work planting trees, fishing, part-time office/clerical work, and studying texts on engineering in his spare time.[142] His experiences at this time tempered his personality to embrace thrift, resolve, and adaptability. Upon his return to England he enrolled as an apprentice at the Lancashire and Yorkshire Locomotive Works. According to Laurence Pritchard, Secretary of the Royal Aeronautical Society at the time, he learned "much heavy

Alliott Verdon Roe. (Library of Congress LCCN2014688439)

An albatross flying over water.

engineering, much human kindness and understanding, while simultaneously earning proficiency certificates from the Mechanics Institute."[143] Aspiring to join the navy, Roe enrolled at King's College to study marine engineering, although the navy didn't feel his grades in subjects other than mathematics and science were good enough. Disheartened, he found work on a British and South African mail steamer, and it was on off-hours aboard the ship that he became interested in aviation, piqued by watching an albatross flying around his ship. He asked himself: "If a bird could glide like this … why should not a man do likewise if he were equipped with [a] suitable apparatus?"[144] He began making and experimenting with models on his final voyage in 1902, after which he worked as a mechanical draughtsman for Brotherton-Crockers Ltd. It was his belief that if he could express his ideas precisely on paper, he would gain the visual vocabulary to express his ideas on manned flight; this work was supplemented and informed by his model experiments.[145]

News of the Wrights' seminal flight at Kitty Hawk didn't reach Roe immediately, communications being much slower then than they are now. When the word did finally arrive in Britain, Roe's astonishment was equally split between the significance of the event and Britain's apathy with regards to it. His frustration culminated with an article he penned to *The Times* in late 1905, about the importance of the Wrights' flight and a prediction that he too would be flying soon.[146] Roe was of course not privy to the negotiations between British leadership and the Wrights, the upshot being that if two Americans could make a flying machine, then certainly someone in England could as well—without such exorbitant cost.

Meanwhile in France, Santos-Dumont was making headlines with his flights—another source of frustration for Roe and other English aviation pioneers; it seemed every country except England was advancing the cause of aviation. Roe's efforts at this time focused on system to induce roll, and was ultimately granted in 1907 UK Patent No. 26,099 for an elevator that could be differentially warped, as well as pitch, both of which were controlled by a single joystick—just like the modern system. This differed from the Wrights whose mechanism actuated these two axes with separate controls.[147]

A "Penny Farthing" bicycle.

Roe's First Plane

At this time, Roe was working out of his brother's carriage house in Putney—it was packed with models, tools, drawings, etc. and he had won a prize of £75 for one of his models at a competition sponsored by the *Daily Mail* and Lord Northcliffe. It is important to remember that this sum in those days represented quite a lot of money. This boosted his confidence such that he planned on building an aircraft that was able to carry a person, which was a full-scale version of his largest model. At full size, the aircraft had a 36-foot wingspan on the top plane and 30 foot on the lower, with an elevator 20-inches wide (per his patent). The warpable elevator was actuated by a metal tube that terminated with a wheel; to bank, the wheel was rotated, for pitch the shaft was pushed/pulled.[148]

He used cheap muslin-backed paper to cover this machine—as he had with his models. The longerons were of bamboo, and the struts were of the same wood that joined the planes. The connections were made via small triangular plates that were riveted to the ends of the struts then fitted to wrap around fittings on the longerons. There were two turnbuckles used, the rest were U-bolts that were tensioned by means of tightening the nuts. The rest of the wires were cut to length and attached with no hardening. The plane had a 9 hp JAP engine mounted as a pusher.[149]

Roe erected a 40 × 40-foot workshop at Brooklands to assemble his new plane. The incentive was a £2500 prize for the first aviator to circle the racetrack. His new plane had a novel four-wheeled undercarriage, with an all-up weight of 450 lbs. In September, he tested it and much to his dismay, it just slowly moved forward due to an underpowered engine and inefficient propeller.[150] Adversity fueled his desire to work harder, and he spent months tweaking the propeller to improve its efficiency. To alert everyone to his objective he painted AVROPLANE above the door to his shed at Brooklands. After taking the prop as far as he could, he finally concluded that the 9 hp engine was just inadequate—the best he could get out of it was enough power to taxi at a walking pace, and his machine had yet to be fitted with a rudder or fin.[151] Seemingly, Roe next removed the engine and tried pulling his machine off the ground with a car. Finally, after various mishaps he was able to get a loaned 24–25 hp Antoinette engine for his airframe.[152] After the new 8-cylinder, 98 lb. engine was installed, he strengthened various parts of the airframe to take the strain of a more powerful engine. Next, he added sub-wings between the two planes to increase lift, thus offsetting the increased weight of the new engine; this was the spark that resulted in his next effort: a triplane. His first flight of about 150 feet in the re-worked plane was made on June 8, 1908;[153] like Sopwith commented, his first flight came as a surprise while engrossed in making routine tests. During this period, George Halse and his brother Arthur worked with Roe on his plane(s).

In September 1908, news of Lt. Thomas Selfridge's death in the Wright Flyer in the U.S. reached England. As a result, the War Office issued criteria required for a military airplane—among them were that it needed to be able to carry an operator and observer each weighing 170 lbs., fuel for four hours, average cruising speed of 25 mph, ceiling of 5,000 feet, steady in flight for observation, must be able to remain uncovered for a month without falling apart, two-hour flights, must be able to glide to safety if engine quits, fuel tank must be near the CofG, must be able to be disassembled and assembled.[154]

The Roe Triplanes

In late 1908, Roe began building his first triplane in his brother's carriage house. He partnered with the Prestwick brothers (makers of the 9 hp JAP engine) who gave him £100 for this project. George Halse helped him and said of Roe, "his confidence in the practicability and future of aviation was undaunted."[155] In spite of the modest funding, Roe had to use the 9 hp engine as he couldn't afford a more powerful engine—as such his triplane was exceedingly lightly built. He secured an order for a second triplane from George Friswell, who

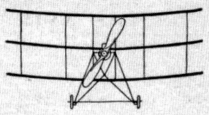

Leading Particulars of the Avroplane.

General Dimensions.—Areas—Main planes, 246 sq. ft. ; elevator, 74¼ sq. ft. ; rudder, 7 sq. ft.

Lengths.—Span, 26 ft. ; chord, 3 ft. 6 ins. ; camber, 1½ ins. ; leverage of rudder, 14 ft. ; skid track, 6 ft. ; overall length, 24 ft. 6 ins.

Angles.—Incidence, variable from 11 to 4 degrees ; dihedral, 1 in 22.

Materials.—Timber, silver spruce struts and spars, ash frame ; fabric, Pegamoid.

Engine.—35-h.p. Green.

Propeller.—Roe ; diameter, 8 ft. ; pitch, 3 ft. ; material, birch.

Weight.—Total flying weight, 550 lbs. ; loading, 17 lbs. per sq. ft.

Speed of Flight.—40 m.p.h.

System of Control.—Warping of planes, elevator and rudder.

Price.—£600.

Drawing of a Roe triplane including specs. (*Flight*)

Replica of a Roe I Triplane.

Below, another view of a replica of an early Roe triplane. Note the way in which the propeller is crafted.

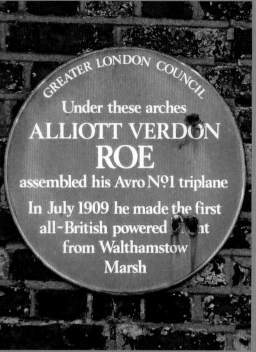

GREATER LONDON COUNCIL

Under these arches
ALLIOTT VERDON
ROE
assembled his Avro Nº1 triplane

In July 1909 he made the first
all~British powered flight
from Walthamstow
Marsh

Railway arches at Walthamstow Marsh railway viaduct.

Plaque commemorating Roe's accomplishment under the railway arches!

A 1908 photograph showing the workshop Roe set up under the railway bridge with partially finished triplane in the foreground.

wanted a 35 hp air-cooled engine. By early 1909, two fuselages, wing parts, and much of the metal fittings were taking shape in his tiny workshop. Realizing the need for more space, he asked the War Office if he could share Farnborough with S. F. Cody—he was turned down as they felt all this aviation experimentation was a national embarrassment.[156] He finally was allowed to build a "workshop" under a railway arch of the Great Eastern Railway at Lea Marshes. In a week, he had the ends of the arches planked in, and although it was dark and dank, he was happy. The Friswell project came to naught and he took the partly finished airframe which he had remodeled then sold it. Roe was penniless again, but was rescued by his brother Humphrey—they made good partners—Roe designing/building the planes, Humphrey worrying about the funding.

In his damp, arched workshop, Roe, Halse, and master woodworker John Bath formed a trio of aircraft builders, and there were several others who helped in varying degrees: Tom Narroway, E. V. B. Fisher, Howard Flanders, George and Martin Sharp.[157] Roe could be seen trying to "hop" his triplane, such that he earned the moniker "The Hopper." Some were amused, others thought him a public nuisance, such as one public

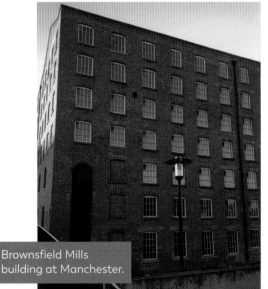

official who attempted to have Roe arrested if he tried to fly![158] At this time, Roe befriended Geoffrey de Havilland and they often exchanged notes about their ideas regarding aircraft design and construction. Roe was determined and persistent, and continued to hop his triplane until he would meet with some mishap; he would then repair and repeat the process. Gradually the hops grew longer until he suffered a bad crash where he was thrown through the middle port main plane.[159]

Louis Blériot crossed the English Channel in July 1909, and in August the Rheims Air Meet was held, cementing the ascendancy of the airplane in the public eye. On the first day of 1910, A. V. Roe & Co. Ltd. was registered with capital supplied by Roe's brother Humphrey, through his holding at Everards, the basement floor of Everards elastic webbing factory, at Brownsfield Mills in Manchester, (which Humphrey managed) was made into a workshop. With the financial backing of his

Brownsfield Mills building at Manchester.

Roe II/"Mercury" triplane exhibited at the Aero and Motor Boat Exhibition, Olympia, March 1910.

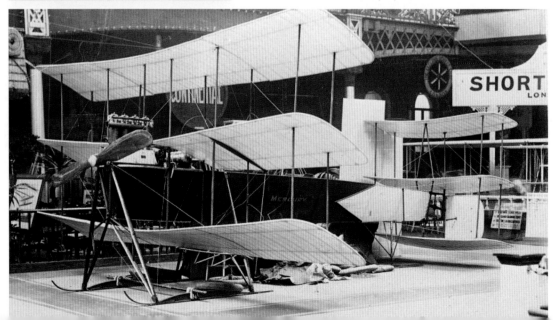

Roe seated in one of his Type I triplane.

Avro IV triplane replica owned by The Shuttleworth
Collection. This replica was originally built for the film
Those Magnificent Men in their Flying Machines and was
subsequently acquired by The Shuttleworth Collection.

Another view of the
Shuttleworth Roe triplane.

The Goupy triplane.

brother, Roe decided it was time get serious so he hired John Parrott as draughtsman. Providentially, an order for a duplicate of the Roe III triplane or "Bull's Eye" was placed, and he began to advertise a fixed cost for finished airplanes.[160]

During the London Olympia Aero and Motor Boat Exhibition of 1910, Roe displayed his Roe II/Mercury triplane, which featured a triangular fuselage sheathed in wood veneers, tandem cockpit, increased wingspan to 26 feet, and a more robust undercarriage with wheels fitted Farman-style. This machine marked the impact of Parrott as he took Roe's idea and refined the engineering of it. Capt. Walter Windham ordered a bigger version of the Mercury that would feature a fixed tailplane with elevators and ailerons on the wings.[161]

Shortly after the Olympia show, it seems obvious that Roe was inspired and influenced by all that he had seen, so he began conceiving of a biplane—the "two-and-a-bit" plane (Roe triplane Mk IV) as it had two full wings and a stubby wing down near the landing gear.[162] Parrott's contribution to this machine was changing production of fittings from folded metal to machined aluminum forgings for all strut attachments. Roe's ribs were standardized and simple: thin top and bottom flanges bent round the spars to a suitable curve separated at intervals by light "distance pieces."[163] The Mk IV had a traditional empennage with rudder and elevators, and an open V-section fuselage. There is a suggestion that it was copied from the Goupy triplane (pictured above) built by the Bleriot factory but of course, these assertions were summarily denied by anyone British.[164] There understandably seems much verbiage expended at this time to point out when something was of British design or innovation; the gap in advances in aviation between Germany and France was keenly felt in England.

The Avro "D" was based on the Mk. IV triplane and made its maiden flight on April 1, 1911, with Howard Pixton as pilot at Brooklands. Howard Pixton was Roe's test pilot at this point.[165] Roe had at this point ascertained the importance of proper placement of the center of gravity with his triplanes through trial and error. The "D"'s arrangement of pilot, passenger and engine up forward was the result of this hard-earned information. The adequate "tail volume" dihedral gave the plane good stability and was reportedly a delight to fly.

The ribs of the "D" were of poplar, spars of English ash, wingtips of bent rattan cane and prop of one piece of kauri pine. The strut junctures to the three fuselage longerons had an efficient clip located by a single bolt to avoid unnecessary piercing of the longerons. The design showed a refinement from Roe's experiences and the fineness of the metal work would characterize Avro in the coming years.[166]

The next biplane made by Roe was commissioned by John Duigan, and featured a single-seat, rectangular (in section) fuselage (instead of triangular). The next plane was a two-seater powered by a 60 hp ENV engine; this was known as the Avro "E" and represented a considerable advance over the "D" model, and was designed by John Parrott who said:

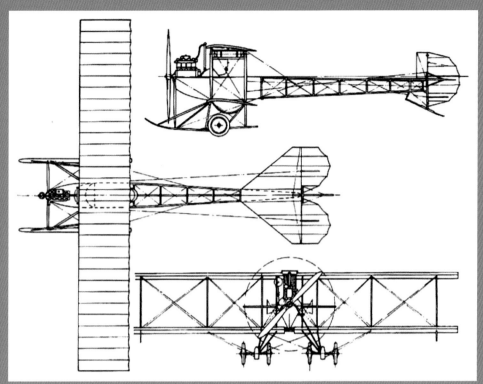

A three-view drawing depicting the Avro Type D. It is easy to see the relationship between this aircraft and the triplanes.

Avro Type D. (Pilot W. D. Beatty)

Every detail has been carefully thought-out, and every line smoothed down. Head resistance is less than any other biplane. The radiators are disposed each outer side of the front cockpit which is under the center section, and thus cuts resistance to a mere nothing. The pilot is located behind the center section struts where he has a splendid view. The undercarriage is entirely new and of much less resistance than the twin skid arrangement of the "D." The machine is mounted on a cross-laminated axle spring to which are fitted two small wheels with metal discs, as on the 1906 biplane. The load is taken by steel struts set transversely V-fashion, and its apex carries a single center skid, which is hinged in the center enabling a certain amount of movement at its nose by compressing a spring fitted to the struts mounted under its engine. The framework of the empennage and rudder is of steel, and all control wires are inside the fuselage. The drum-like fabric covering is produced by treating it with a dope called Emaillite.[167]

Up until the advent of Emaillite, doping of airframes was problematic using sago (a starch extracted from palm trees) which kept fabric tight while dry but if there was rain or dew the fabric became slack and soggy again. In early 1911, Pegamoid was popular albeit briefly, as it too would become slack. This was replaced by rubberized

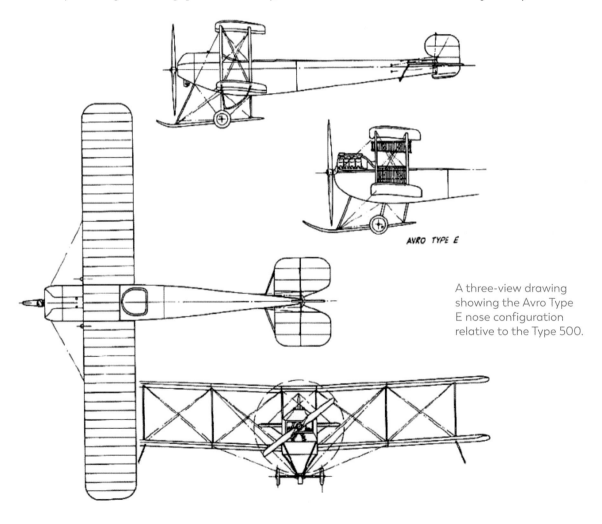

AVRO TYPE E

A three-view drawing showing the Avro Type E nose configuration relative to the Type 500.

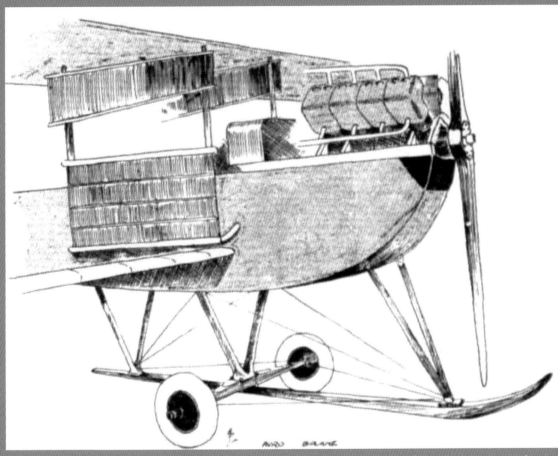

Illustration of the Type E nose showing the radiator and engine configuration. (*Flight*, March 30, 1912)

Advertisements for Emaillite dope and Avro. (*The Aero*, December 1912)

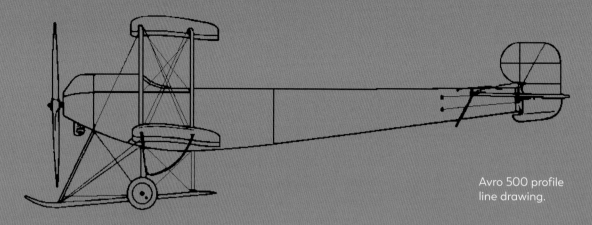

Avro 500 profile
line drawing.

Avro 500.

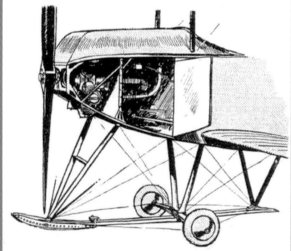

A detailed illustration of the nose of the Avro
500 showing interior engine arrangement.
(*Flight*, February 15, 1913)

A close-up view of the front of the skid of Avro 500
which featured a shock-absorbing tip that was set up
with a spring. (*Flight*, February 15, 1913)

fabric which passed in popularity as well. Mid-1911 Emaillite from France, like the British Cellon (acetate lacquer), was derived from chemical study by Dr. Eisengrun in Berlin.[168] These new cellulose acetate dopes were revolutionary as they were impervious to moisture and could adhere fabric to itself permanently. Penrose stated that at this juncture, the dope was more important than duralumin.[169]

The Roe E was the first of Roe's aircraft to go into production. It was first flown in March 1912. The War Office ordered three type "E" planes from Roe, and these planes featured improvements over the prototype; the fuselage was deeper and the lower wings lined up with the lower longerons. It had celluloid panels fitted to the bottom of the fuselage to aid in observation. The Gnome engine was fitted to a spider plate that spanned the forward longerons. At this time, Roy Chadwick was hired to evaluate stresses on the airframes. Chadwick was given the task of re-drafting the "E" to form a new version which became known as the Avro 500.[170] In all, 18 Avro 500s were ordered—mostly for the RFC. The previous year, Roy Chadwick had been hired as Roe's personal assistant, and the firm's draughtsman to aid in professionalizing the drawings necessary for production and selling a particular design to British leadership. For the first time, Roe had neatly lined ink drawings of his aircraft instead of pencil sketches.

The first plane to be depicted in professional drawings was the Roe F monoplane which may have been influenced by the Levavasseur Antoinette. From its profile view it looked like a symmetrical airfoil with a tiny rudder. The type F (and type G biplane) were the world's first aircraft that were built with enclosed crew accommodation in 1912; neither progressing beyond the prototype stage. In the latter part of 1911 they built their first monoplane—a commission from Lt. R. Burga, a Portuguese officer. This aircraft was scheduled for testing in early 1912, and was a two-seater featuring a 50 hp Gnome powered two-seater. Its main planes (wingspan 34 feet) were located just below the upper longerons. These wings were braced from the V strut landing gear ("D" style), and had an empennage of the "D" as well. The nose of this machine was to inspire the development of the Avro 500 (as the "D" with the Gnome had been renamed).[171]

The Avro works at Brownsfield Mills, Manchester, had developed into a considerable factory due to profits from the flying school and success of the Avro "D" tractor biplane. These successes inspired Roe's financial backers to grant more capital for expansion. A new assembly hall was built as well as separate shops for woodworking, metalsmithing, wing and fuselage construction, and a covering shop completely staffed by women.

The Avro Type F. Note the fully enclosed cockpit which would become the norm much later in aircraft development.

In Profile
Avro 504K

Avro 504K: (E3259) No. 33 (HD) Squadron, RAF; Kirton-on-Lindsay, UK; September 1918. The Avro 504K was the most successful version of the Avro 504.

RONNY
BAR
ronnybarprofiles@gmail.com

The Avro 504

The Type 500 was the point of departure for the Avro 504, which was first flown in September 1913. A small number were bought by the War Office before the outbreak of World War I, and the type saw some front-line service in the early months of the war, but it is best known as a training aircraft, serving in this role until 1933. Production of the 504 lasted 20 years and totaled 8,340 aircraft, which were produced by several factories including Hamble, Failsworth, Miles Platting and Newton Heath.

Roy Chadwick, working away in his small office, refined the sketch by Roe of the 504 that was drawn in spring 1913.[172] That sketch still exists and includes fitting details, cockpit arrangement, adjustable windscreen, and a roller screen (like a window shade) to cover the passenger cockpit when not in use. R. J. Parrott said to the press about the new plane:

> In April construction commences on our new type to supersede the Type 500 ... principal differences ... heavy wing stagger for increased efficiency of downward and forward view; increased span and chord; a better wing section [airfoil]; improved fuselage streamlining; fitting of a unique undercarriage.[173]

The "unique undercarriage" to which Parrott referred was a telescoping set of tubes sprung with rubber—a departure from the leaf-spring shock absorbers of the 500. The fuselage was a little narrower than the cowling for the Gnome so blisters were designed to blend one into another. It had a semi-circular, full-flying rudder. The

Above, a replica Avro 504 E3273 (G-ADEV) of The Shuttleworth Collection.

An archival image of Avro 504 in the field.

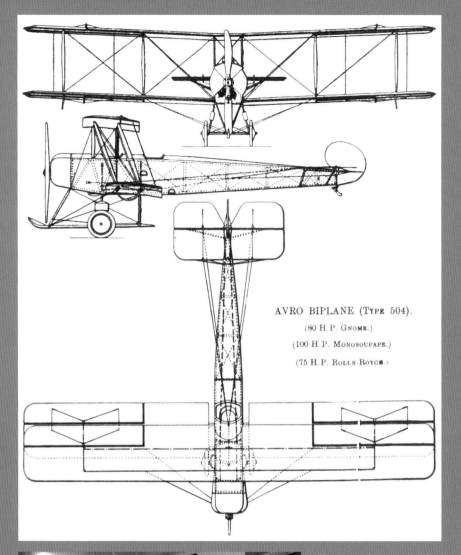

AVRO BIPLANE (TYPE 504).

(80 H.P. GNOME.)

(100 H.P. MONOSOUPAPE.)

(75 H.P. ROLLS-ROYCE.)

Above, a three-view drawing of the Avro 504.

John Gaertner's beautiful replica of an Avro 504; the fuselage is mostly finished. (Image courtesy of Blue Swallow Aircraft)

The seat for the 504 is almost finished and is fitted to a mockup to insure proper fit and alignment. (Image courtesy of Blue Swallow Aircraft)

wings had ailerons that warped; the inboard end was fixed, the outer had increased chord and was warped by means of wires. The plane was built at Roe's new plant at Clifton St., Miles Platting, Manchester. The new plant had enlarged design/drafting offices for Roy Chadwick, Frank Vernon (stress work), Roe in a small office near the drafting office, Chief Engineer, and downstairs an office for his brother Humphrey, Managing Director.[174]

John Gaertner, sole proprietor of Blue Swallow Aircraft in Virginia, has spent many years studying and restoring vintage aircraft. Near and dear to John is the Avro 504, in fact he made this aircraft the subject of his Master's thesis! John noted that since Roe worked for a railroad, he was keenly aware of the size of a standard English rail crate, and so planned the modular nature of the 504 accordingly; it would fit neatly in one of these crates. The fuselage was meant to split in half such that it would fit in a crate as well. When I asked him about the peculiar frontal skid, which I presumed was to prevent nose-overs, he commented that in those days, a custom handmade propeller was a big investment in time and money, so the skid prevented the propeller from being damaged, add to that the fact that the engine cost as much as the plane, finally the skid helped push down tall grass making a landing roll out easier.

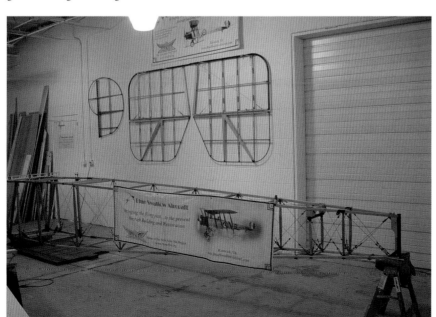

Fuselage, horizontal stabilizer and elevators, and rudder are awaiting assembly. (Image courtesy of Blue Swallow Aircraft)

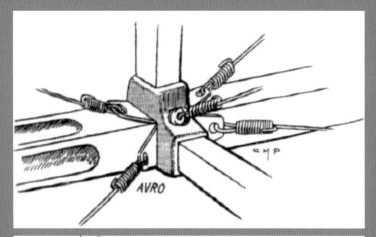

This illustration shows the configuration of the longeron to strut and cross piece fitting for the Avro 504. Note how piercing of the timbers is kept to a minimum to avoid weakening them. (*Flight*, December 6, 1913 p. 1326)

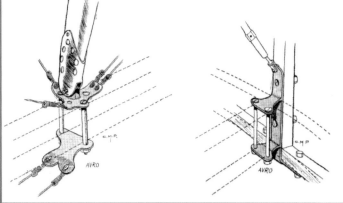

Details of the interplane to wing spar joint, and lower wing spar to fuselage joint fittings. Note well how the main load-bearing timbers are protected from weakness by little or no drilling. (*Flight*, December 6, 1913 p. 1325)

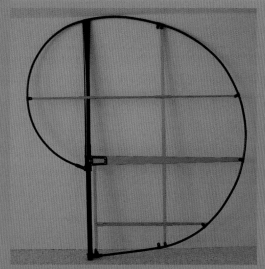

A close-up of the rudder construction which is a composite of steel and spruce. Note the fineness of the metal fittings—tiny tangs to which the spruce formers are fastened, and the delicacy of the proportions of all the components. (Image courtesy of Blue Swallow Aircraft)

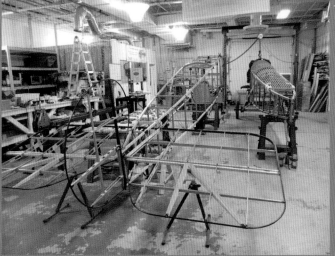

The fuselage and empennage assembled. Note the amount of spruce in the empennage; an effort to keep the tail light, yet strong. The elevators on the 504 are generous. (Image courtesy of Blue Swallow Aircraft)

John Gaertner: Building the Avro 504

Aircraft restorer, builder, and museum professional John Gaertner set out at an early age to work on antique aircraft with no idea of where that was going to take him. He spent 14 years in the aviation museum world, so he could learn and gain the experience for ultimately working on his own planes and other people's planes. Although not particularly interested in WWI aircraft per se, he is passionate about early, pre-WWII aircraft that had a profound impact on aviation history—a prime example being the Avro 504. The skills John developed over the years were crucial to the processes required to restore aircraft of this period. John developed these skills through formal learning and trial and error on his own. His museum and educational experiences have built on one another and John has continued to increase and develop his skill set over many years. Currently John owns and operates Blue Swallow Aircraft LLC in Free Union, Virginia: www.blueswallowaircraft.com.

John continued by noting that Roe was very cheap so he designed his own steel three-piece turnbuckles because the ones favored by most builders were very expensive barrels of turned brass, with left and right hand threads. His turnbuckle design had two simple Swiss Screw turned threaded parts and a steel pressed formed saddle in only two weights and only four or five sizes. A. V. Roe made more money selling his patented turnbuckles than he ever did making airplanes. They were used in everything for years and copied by numerous other foreign manufacturers.

The 504 prototype was flown at Brooklands by Freddy Raynham in late July 1913. The warping ailerons were found to be nominally effective so were replaced by standard hinged ones. Spruce interplane struts were refined to be a bit thicker in the middle and well-shaped and tapered at the ends—the originals proved too spindly. A new spider-plate was fabricated for the Gnome, enabling it to receive a round cowling. This in turn was faired with a semi-circular triangular blister. Penrose noted that Roe developed the proportions of the 504 intuitively.[175]

Flight wrote that, "Three things at least stand to the credit of A. V. Roe: the development of the first successful triplane, the application of the monoplane-type body on multiplane machines, and the construction of commercial airplanes for men of moderate means."[176]

The plywood turtle deck has been fitted to the formers atop the upper longerons. (Image courtesy of Blue Swallow Aircraft)

The tailskid for the 504—a four-legged support structure fastened to the lower longerons, supporting a central steel post, that the ash tailskid pivots upon and is set up with springs to the upper longeron near the stabilizer. (Image courtesy of Blue Swallow Aircraft)

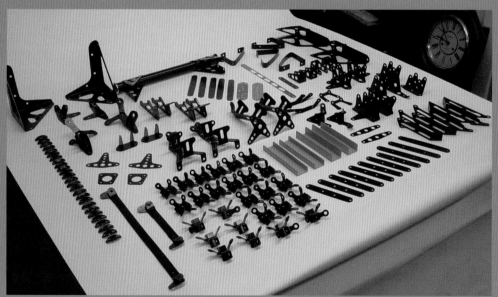

The fittings for the 504 as beautifully fabricated by John Gaertner. Note the fineness of the articulation of each fitting; just enough strength where needed but no more to keep the fittings lightweight. (Image courtesy of Blue Swallow Aircraft)

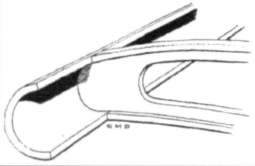

A stack of wing ribs for the 504. Note the bullnose at the forward end of the ribs, which will seat on the interior cove of the shaped leading edge. (Image courtesy of Blue Swallow Aircraft)

The fitting of a hollowed leading edge to the forward end of rib webs. (*Flight*, February 7, 1914)

The wing panel of the 504 replica (G-ADEV) of The Shuttleworth Collection that has been covered and doped. Note the fuselage in the background awaiting recovering.

The main landing skid has been stack-laminated and glued with epoxy; a modern concession but otherwise a perfect replica of the original; complete with spindled-out grooves to save weight. (Image courtesy of Blue Swallow Aircraft)

The finished landing skid. Apparently Roe opted to abandon the spring-loaded pivoting skid of the 500, in favor of a fixed end on the 504. (Image courtesy of Blue Swallow Aircraft)

A main gear strut for the 504; note the telescoping steel tube arrangement and the cross pieces to which the shock cords were set up. (Image courtesy of Blue Swallow Aircraft)

Below, a 504 replica taking off in New Zealand.

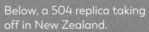

A replica Avro 504 E3273 (G-ADEV) of The Shuttleworth Collection.

Another Avro 504 replica taking off—the aircraft is owned by Eric Verdon Roe, great-grandson of Alliott Verdon Roe.

Below, a photo showing an Avro 504K with a Foster mount and Lewis gun atop the main plane.

Above, another ad for Avro—note how the logo has been finalized and changed from the earlier version. Featured prominently is a silhouette of their signature plane: the 504. (*The Aeroplane*, May 9, 1917)

| Sopwith Aviation Company

The Sopwith aircraft dominated the British aviation scene throughout the war with a very successful line of fighters that were basically all derived from the same essential design beginning with the Tabloid. Like Fokker, Thomas Sopwith found something that worked well for him and his company and stuck with it, each design improving on the last, yet they were all related. Seemingly, his company was characterized by inventiveness, a passion for the work and compassion for those who worked for him, and humor—Tommy Sopwith was a character!

Thomas O. M. Sopwith was born into a privileged environment in London in early 1888. Although Tom was mechanically minded and liked balloons, cars, and motorcycles, the Wrights' flight had little impact on him (so he said). At the time, he was far more interested in sailing and country activities.

Sopwith and his friend V. W. Eyre jointly owned a 166-ton schooner named *Neva*. Sopwith wanted to install a new engine in the boat, and this led him to Fred Sigrist, who worked at Parsons Motor Co., forging a connection with a man who would be integral to the future Sopwith Aviation Company. Bill Eyre hired him and paid him a weekly salary, such that he left his job in 1910.[177]

Bramson says the August 1910 Moisant flight (crossing the English Channel with a passenger and a kitten) fueled Sopwith's imagination, such that he visited Brooklands, where for a small fee you could fly in a Farman piloted by Frenchman Gustav Blondeau. Sopwith had this to say:

> I went down to Brooklands where Maurice Hewlett had brought a Farman over from France and was giving joyrides around Brooklands at a fiver at [a] time. So I thought I would have a fiver's worth which consisted of two circuits inside the track at Brooklands. And I think that was the start of the bug.[178]

John B. Moisant and Mademoiselle Fifi.

Sopwith's first airplane was a Howard T. Wright (no relation to the Wright brothers) Avis monoplane that he bought for £630, which was powered by a 40 hp ENV engine. Working at Howard Wright was Jack Pollard—a fortuitous encounter, as he would eventually join the Sopwith team.[179]

In writing about his first flight, Sopwith commented that you learned to taxi first then gradually increase speed as you traveled in a straight line. He said: "As it happened in several cases, one's first flight was by mistake, because you looked over the side and found the ground had gone—so you had to try and get back again."[180] After a few mishaps and much practice trying to fly one circuit, he concluded that his 40 hp engine was underpowered, so he replaced it with a Howard Wright biplane fitted with 60 hp engine.[181] He said: "I seized every opportunity to get into the air and by the time I had ten hours flying behind me, I began to feel I was a really experienced pilot."[182]

Sopwith made a trip to the U.S. to do various demonstration flights, which was not well received by some of the American press, who noted that British pilots were making more money than American aviators on an invention that originated in the U.S. The Wright brothers were not exactly thrilled to see Sopwith as they felt his

1910 Howard Wright biplane "Manurewa" making a flight from Glenora Park, Papakura, Auckland, c. 1911.

machine was violating their patents. The Wrights actually filed a Bill of Complaint in court, aimed at preventing Sopwith from making further flights in America on the grounds that his British-designed and built Howard Wright biplane infringed on their patents. This of course was remedied when Sopwith bought a plane from the Wrights![183] Sopwith had this to say about it:

> Speaking from a mechanical standpoint, I think the Wright machine is a monstrosity. I don't see how it could be any worse and still it seems to fly very reliably. As you say in this country it seems "to get there" but that chain from the motor to the propellers is a very bad arrangement.[184]

The American competitions had been a great experience for Tommy Sopwith. He had won a large appreciative audience, had competed against some of the finest pilots in the world, and had won on many occasions.

Back in England, the aviation scene was improving, and this was entirely the result of private enterprise, for the state exhibited a calculated indifference to the rapid development of airplanes, as it likely still thought of itself as a naval power with a strong navy as the pre-eminent war machine. One of the most effective entrepreneurs was Claude Grahame-White. Early in 1910, he had founded the London Aerodrome at Hendon, which in time became a fashionable entertainment spot for the public. There were joyrides, aerobatics, air races, and low-level passes. Although rivals at many competitions, Sopwith and Grahame-White had become good friends; or at least engendered a mutual respect.[185]

Using his European and U.S. prize money, Sopwith set up the Sopwith School of Flying at Brooklands in 1912. Sopwith said that he was "teaching people to do something I knew very little about."[186] The school had a Blériot two-seater, Howard Wright monoplane, Burgess-Wright biplane (modified for instruction), and the Martin and Handasyde monoplane. Fred Sigrist managed the daily aircraft maintenance engineering while Sopwith and Fred Raynham gave flying lessons.

As mentioned already, although the Admiralty and War Office showed little initial interest in aviation, they did manage to set up the Army Air Battalion in 1911 as a way to appease mounting public and political support for a military air presence in England. Officers would learn at a private school like Sopwith's, then after receiving their ticket, go to the Central Flying School at Upavon on Salisbury Plain. The most famous student to pass through there was Major Hugh Trenchard who wanted to become a pilot in the Royal Flying Corps (founded in 1912). Brooklands was the hub for aviation and car racing with various huts set up to serve as flying schools. Trenchard decided to learn at Sopwith's. Sopwith agreed to teach him to fly in 10 days for the fee of 75 pounds.[187] Apparently, Sopwith felt Trenchard wasn't a great pilot!

Howard Pixton in an Avro biplane. Pixton was Roe's first test pilot.

Harry Hawker, May 1919.

Howard Pixton—an outstanding aviator who flew for the Bristol school at Brooklands—next became acquainted with Sopwith and would prove to be a huge asset at the company in the years to come. Harry Kauper and Harry Hawker were two Australians who had a profound impact on Sopwith. The former would become the works manager, and the latter would become Sopwith's chief test pilot.[188]

Interest in aviation had risen sufficiently in England by 1912, such that there were 16 civil flying schools operating in Britain and, over the course of a year, they trained 181 pilots.[189] By 1913, people were complaining about "unscrupulous elements" cashing in on the flying craze; bogus flying school operators took money in advance for training, then spent the money themselves on flying lessons![190] By this time Fred Sigrist induced Sopwith to stop teaching and start building airplanes—the timing was perfect.

In spite of modest gains in acceptance of aviation in England, France and Germany were racing ahead in support of their designers and pilots. The Brits were floored by the support France had for its aviators and aviation in general. British manufacturers met with Colonel J. E. B. Seely of the War Office to whom they stated that Britain was not only being left behind by Germany and France—it was not even in the race![191] English leadership finally decided that military trials would be held on Salisbury Plain during 1912, after which suitable aircraft would be ordered for the purpose of training 100 officers and pilots. The total prize money for the winners was set at £11,000. In contrast, French authorities had awarded £53,000 in awards.[192]

Sopwith flew the Coventry Ordnance Works biplane which was a grotesque and awful airplane—the only decent plane was designed by de Havilland but since he was working for the government-funded Royal Aircraft Factory, it was not allowed to participate. The competition was won by S. F. Cody, although none of the aircraft distinguished themselves.

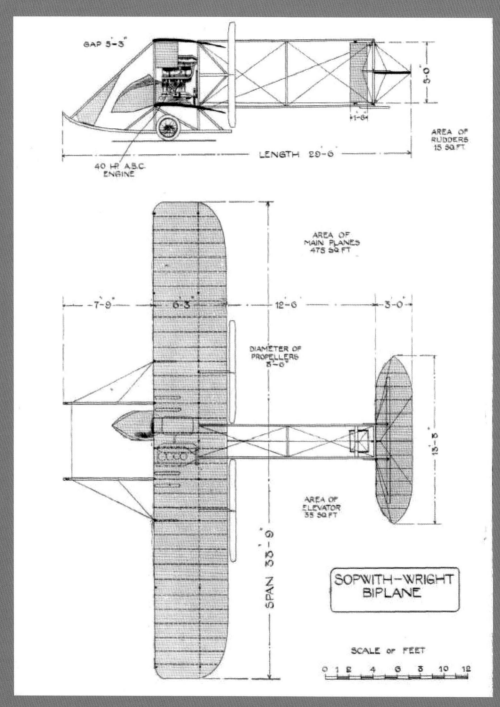

The Sopwith-Wright biplane which featured an off-center nacelle to give the pilot some protection and streamlining. (*Flight*, November 23, 1912)

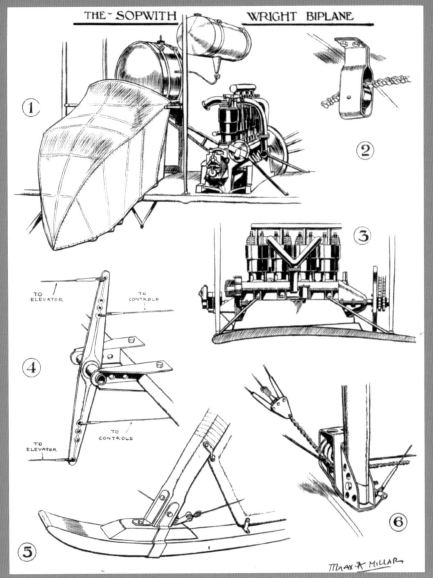

THE SOPWITH WRIGHT BIPLANE

① ② ③ ④

TO ELEVATOR

TO CONTROLS

TO CONTROLS

TO ELEVATOR

⑤ ⑥

Max A. Millar

Left, construction details of the Sopwith Wright biplane. (*Flight*, November 23, 1912)

Below, the Sopwith "Hybrid" was aptly named; it combined Burgess-Wright type wings, a modified Blériot fuselage, and other borrowed components. Most importantly, it resembled an airplane in the modern sense with a fuselage, empennage, and pair of wings. (Kingston Aviation website, www.kingstonaviation.org)

Kip Lankeneau: Building the Sopwith 1½ Strutter

Kip had this to say about his life-long passion for aviation, which led him to building aircraft:

I grew up in southeastern Michigan in a family where my father owned an airplane (J-3) before an automobile. As a small child, I would sit on my father's lap and "fly" our Stinson Voyager. We rarely took driving vacations, flying all over North America was the norm. Our family was part of "The Flyers Club," a group started by my father and several others at the behest of our local Beechcraft dealer (we were flying a 35 Bonanza at the time). We had monthly social meetings to plan our weekend trips, frequently flying in formation. Dawn Patrol pancake breakfasts were a normal part of life, and I was surrounded by pilots and airplanes old and new. My mother was also a pilot, an active member of the 99s, and a frequent competitor in women's air races.

I earned my PPL sophomore year at Michigan State, and took a V35A Bonanza to school as a junior, and flew it to Florida for spring break. We had a grass strip at home and I would fly home every Wednesday (weather permitting) and have lunch while my grandmother did my laundry. Many pilot friends wanted to land on our grass strip, but many were afraid. So, I'd meet them at a nearby airport and fly their plane over and back, just so they could say they'd done it. I never logged these short flights, but can tell you that I have briefly flown an extensive variety of aircraft. By my senior year, I'd earned commercial, instrument and multi-engine ratings.

Another great influence was my grandfather, who'd been hired by Edsel Ford and was a senior Ford Motor Company executive. Growing up,

we spent a lot of time at Greenfield Village and Henry Ford Museum, where with my natural mechanical ability and curiosity, I learned how to work on and operate many types of early machinery, from steam engines to automobiles, sawmills, printing presses, glass blowing, well you can just let your imagination run wild. At home, I would replicate many of Edison's early experiments and also consumed much time making cannons, firearms, a hang glider (Rogalo wing), not to mention flying model airplanes and rockets (my family tree is littered with inventors and gunsmiths). I was a member of the Antique Automobile Club of America by age five and an Eagle Scout from a time when you still needed to learn semaphore, Morse and pioneering.

A voracious reader, I woke up every morning with a book in my hands, with history and technology being the primary fare, but also with an interest in Jules Verne. By age 10 I'd read *No Parachute* by Arthur Gould Lee, and would scour libraries and bookshops, frequently special-ordering obscure titles.

As to your question; What inspires you to do this type of work? It's not my work, it's who I am. History is not something to be read, it's something to be experienced.

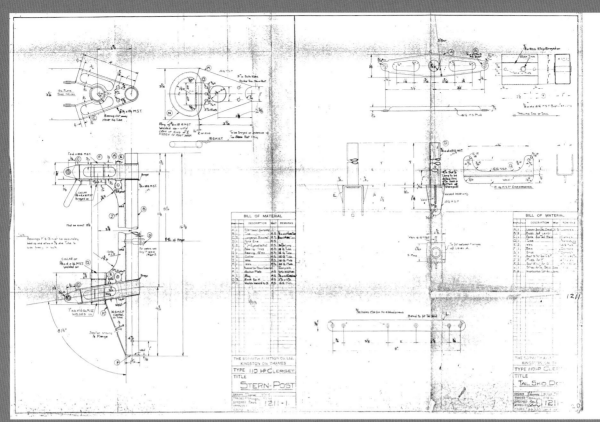

Sopwith drawings showing the complex adjustable incidence gear on the horizontal stabilizer. (Image courtesy of KipAero)

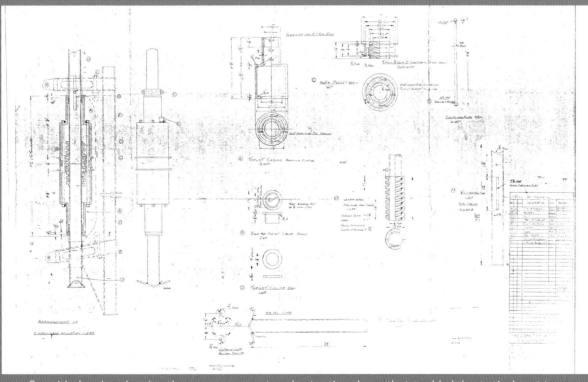

Sopwith drawing showing the worm gear post and actuating sleeve that enabled the vertical post to raise and lower the aft edge of the horizontal stabilizer. (Image courtesy of KipAero)

KipAero's replica of the Sopwith 1 ½ Strutter taking off. (Image courtesy of KipAero)

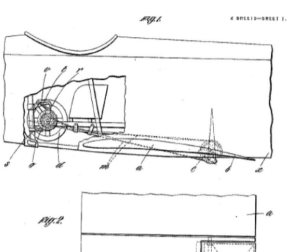

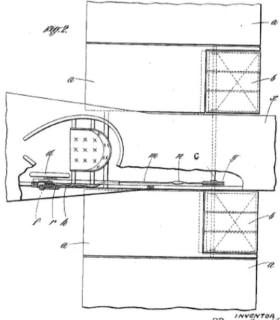

By late May 1916, thoughts at Sopwith turned to improving takeoff performance while simultaneously increasing load capacity. This resulted in an increase in wingspan, larger ailerons, and Sopwith's patented "Wind Brakes for Aeroplanes" which acted as flaps do in modern aircraft. These were actuated by a turning a handle in the cockpit which rotated the flap, which was hinged to the aft spar, downward. These flaps could be set to different degrees on each wing, thus enabling the pilot to trim the aircraft.[227] The Strutter "Bus" was one of the first aircraft to be fitted with air brakes (which pilots didn't like due to the vibration they caused) and it had a maximum speed of only 98 mph and it remained in production until 1923.[228]

On June 6, 1915, Hawker flew the "Sigrist Bus" and reached 18,393 feet establishing a new British altitude record, with a speed speculated to have been around 90 mph.[229]In the early summer of 1916, a new machine was signed off from the

Drawing of the Strutter's air brake that was prepared for the U.S. patent application.

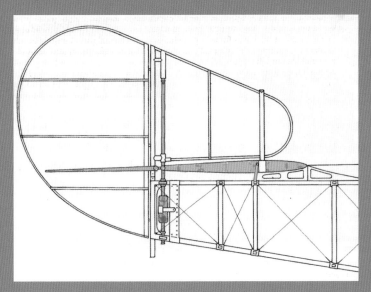

An illustration showing the empennage indicating the adjustable portion of the tail. (Kingston Aviation website, www.kingstonaviation.org)

KipAero's Strutter showing this assembly as fabricated. (Image courtesy of KipAero)

KipAero's fuselage of their Strutter with Gnome rotary engine that was built new to factory specs. (Image courtesy of KipAero)

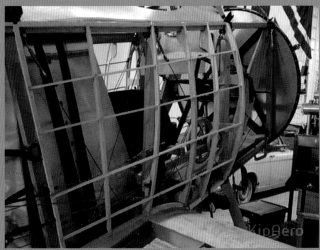

Detail of the cheek and cockpit of the KipAero Strutter. (Image courtesy of KipAero)

Archival image of an original Strutter at the Sopwith factory. Note the variable incidence wheel on the port side, and the trim tab wheel on the starboard. (Kingston Aviation website, www.kingstonaviation.org).

Experimental Department and was given the name of LCT (Land Clerget Tractor). This aircraft had differences from the "Bus" in that although retaining the W-shaped cabane struts, its mainplanes were of equal span, and had a lower center section, the spars from which passed through the fuselage. It also had a more powerful engine—a 110 hp Clerget that was fully cowled with formed aluminum, giving it a functional and clean look. The cowling was thusly faired into the fuselage by a series of diminishing cambered formers that blended the curve of the cowling into the slab sides of the box-girder fuselage framing. This system became standard for the Pup, the Triplane, and the Camel. Obviously, it was a cost-effective way to make this transition as it was used on much of Sopwith's aircraft. It was anticipated the plane would have a high landing speed given its clean lines, thus, airbrakes were designed and fitted to the roots of the lower wings (see figure and the patent appendix). It also featured another patented invention—an adjustable tailplane (UK Patent No. 126,031)—enabling the pilot to re-trim the plane once ordnance had been dropped. Moreover, the capacious fuel tank, which held 40 gallons, would also alter trim as the fuel was consumed.[230]

In 1916, the Strutter was rolled out. It was the first Sopwith design to be mass-produced on a grand scale by subcontractors.[231] The French built no fewer than 4,200 of them; Britain produced even more. Interestingly, the British Army was not impressed with them; not so with the Admiralty. Deliveries started in February of that year, and soon demand exceeded supply such that Vickers, and Ruston and Proctor built them. Another Sopwith innovation was the invention of shift work to meet demand for the Strutters.[232]

KipAero is a company dedicated "to assist the vintage aviation enthusiast by providing the parts and expertise needed to accurately build, restore, repair and maintain your vintage airplane." Their contact information is available at kipaero.com and they offer fully built or kits of the Camel, Strutter, or Pup. Their Strutter is shown in the "bones" on p.131.

The Pup

It was common knowledge that Harry Hawker chalked the outline of a "runabout" on the workshop floor at Kingston. The result was an aircraft labeled SLTBP (Davis proposed: "Sopwith Light Tractor Biplane") and drawings for this new plane were ready by late 1915.[233] Construction of the first "Pup" (so named as it looked like a "pup" of the larger Strutter[234]) followed quickly after the SLTBP. The influence of Hawker's "runabout" was obvious on the new plane. The Pup tailplane and mainplanes, although built differently, retained the plan form of the SLTBP with wing tips that raked aft. The Pup had a wider center section and corresponding cabane struts that angled outboard.[235] Most importantly, ailerons were fitted to all four wings (like the Strutter), thus underscoring the end of the structural absurdity of wing-warping.

On February 9, 1916, the Experimental Department of Sopwith passed a scout designed by Herbert Smith (his Strutter was already in production). The new scout resembled the Strutter except it was more compact and had an 80 hp Le Rhône. In essence, it was the military iteration of a small stunt plane that was built in 1915 for Harry Hawker.

Since Sopwith was a contractor to the Admiralty in 1916, the first five Pups were sent to the RNAS and were equipped with 80 hp Clerget engines.[236] Pups to the RNAS were built by Sopwith and the Beardmore & Co. The first 11 were equipped with Clerget engines; after that they were all 80 hp Le Rhônes.[237]

Sopwith had this say about the Pup:

> The Pup was pre-Camel. It was a dear little machine with an 80 hp Gnome and, as a flying machine, it was sort of machine you could give to anybody and he couldn't hurt himself. It did everything you wanted it to do—had no tricks or vices.[238]

The Pup was based very much on the Tabloid, and it took the aviation world by storm. The Pup's particular advantage was it was able to maintain height in a dogfight; something few other planes could do at the time.[239] Also importantly, the Pup was the only Allied fighter of the period capable of climbing high enough to attack a Zeppelin. This is corroborated by the fact that the undersides of some Pups were doped light blue.[240] Pups were used throughout the war with some 2,000 being built.

The fuselage was framed in the typical box-girder and wire-braced construction that was used in the Strutter, including the ash longerons and vertical struts of spruce. Mainplanes were of spruce ribs and spars, but wing tips were made from steel tubing, as was much of the empennage. The Pups had 18.5 gallon fuel tanks, and 5 gallon oil tanks which were mounted above and behind the engine in the fuselage. Pups consumed around six gallons of fuel per hour at 8,000 feet at 1,175 rpm. Castor oil consumption was around ten pints/hr., cowling and cheek panels were made from sheet aluminum, and the turtle deck was made from plywood. Leading edges, ribs, riblets and compression timbers were wood.[241] A single Vickers machine gun was mounted atop the turtle deck immediately in front of the pilot. The gun had a patented padded windscreen built in, although some preferred just a padded gun breech, whereas others still liked a wider windscreen at the forward end of

The SLTBP prototype at Brooklands. (Kingston Aviation website, www.kingstonaviation.org)

The Pup prototype at Brooklands. The Pup earned its name when placed next to a Strutter which made it look like the young offspring of the larger plane. (Kingston Aviation website, www. kingstonaviation.org)

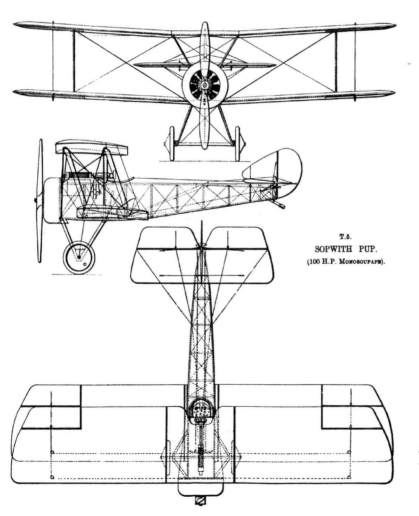

T.5.
SOPWITH PUP.
(100 H.P. Monosoupape).

A three-view drawing of the Sopwith Pup.

The 80 hp Le Rhône 9C engine, firewall, and diagonal engine/landing gear support strut of the Sopwith Pup, Fleet Air Arm Museum, Yeovilton.

The rebuilt Sopwith Pup from The Shuttleworth Collection taking off.

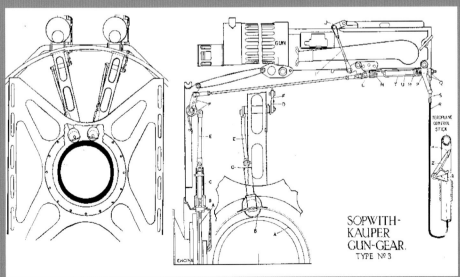

Sopwith-Kauper interrupter gear, 1917.

the coaming.[242] The gun-synchronizing system was the Sopwith-Kauper interrupter gear, on later aircraft the Scarff-Dibovski or Constantinesco (C.C.) synchronizing mechanisms were fitted.[243]

James McCudden found that a Pup in the right hands could be a good match for an Albatros D.III:

I realized that the Sopwith could outmaneuver any Albatros, no matter how good the pilot was … when it came to maneuvering, the Sopwith Scout would turn twice to an Albatros' once.[244]

Oliver Stewart described a Pup as such:

The perfect flying machine. This is the term which the Sopwith triplane nearly fulfilled and which the Sopwith Pup did fulfill. As a military aircraft, it had certain shortcomings, but as a flying machine—a machine which gave a high return in speed and climb for a given expenditure of horse power, which had well-balanced, powerful controls, which was stable enough but not too stable, which was sensitive enough without being too sensitive, and which obeyed its pilot in a way that eventually secured his lasting admiration and affection—the Sopwith Pup was and still is without superior.[245]

The Pup had wide chord wings with forward swept tips and ailerons on both sets of wings.

In Profile
Sopwith Pup

Sopwith Pup: Flt Sub Lt. A. W. Carter, No. 3 (N)
Squadron, RNAS; Marieux, France; April 1917.

ronnybarprofiles@gmail.com

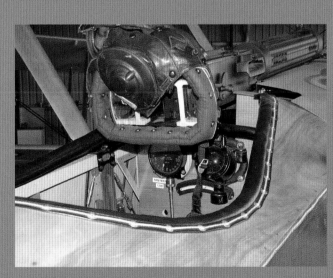

Above, the Pup's cockpit showing the padded windscreen
that was mounted to the after side of the breach of the
Vickers gun.

The Pup's cockpit. (Darren Harbar)

In Profile
Sopwith Triplane

Sopwith Triplane: Flt Lt. A. R. Arnold, No. 8 (N)
Squadron, RNAS; St Eloi, France; July 1918.

RONNY
BAR

ronnybarprofiles@gmail.com

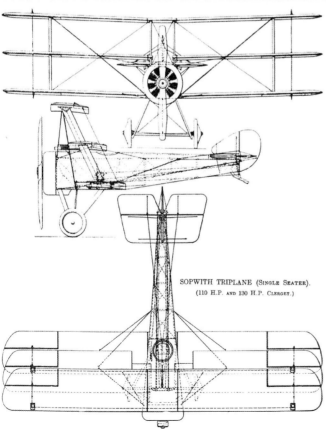

SOPWITH TRIPLANE (Single Seater).
(110 H.P. and 130 H.P. Clerget.)

The Triplane

Triplane experiments began as early as 1908 by Hans Grade in Germany and Goupy in France, and two years later in England by A. V. Roe. Soon afterward the triplane fell out of favor, and the focus shifted to monoplanes—likely due to the success of the Blériot XI. Triplanes had appeal due to their high lifting capacity (especially with an underpowered engine in the case of Roe) and shorter wingspan. This design feature kept interest in the triplane alive. The genesis of the Sopwith triplane was spurred by the desire for excellent pilot visibility, rate of climb, and maneuverability.[246] It was the brainchild of Sopwith's Chief Engineer Herbert Smith. The narrow chord (3 feet, 3 inches) of the three wings provided plenty of lift yet afforded excellent downward visibility. The central wing was nearly level with the pilot's eyes and as such obscured only the thickness of this wing, which was fairly

A three-view drawing of the Sopwith Triplane.

The Sopwith triplane in the bones at the Sopwith factory, Canbury Park Road, April 1917. (Kingston Aviation website, www.kingstonaviation.org)

The fuselage of the first triplane in New Works, May 1916. (Kingston Aviation website, www.kingstonaviation.org)

The cockpit of the Sopwith triplane; note the fuel pressurizing prop-driven device on port cabane strut.

slender when compared to the Fokker Dr.1. In addition, ailerons were fitted to all three wings which made roll rate very responsive and light. The fuselage and empennage were similar to the Sopwith Pup, but with a different cabane strut structure (one wide strut port and starboard) to allow attachment of the three planes. The horizontal stabilizer had variable incidence, which was actuated by a wheel to the pilot's right—just like the Strutter. When properly trimmed it allowed the pilot to fly hands free. The introduction of a smaller 8-foot span horizontal stabilizer and elevators in February 1917, made pitch response more stable and less sensitive. Only 147 triplanes were built, but they did inspire the Germans to waste valuable time designing one of their own; had they pursued the D.VII or D.VIII sooner, it wouldn't have turned the tide in Germany's favor, but it would have cost the lives of many more Allied pilots.

The triplane was initially powered by the 110 hp Clerget 9Z 9-cylinder rotary engine, but most production examples were fitted with the 130 hp Clerget 9B rotary.[247] The first Sopwith triplane (prototype N500) was first flown on May 28, 1916 at the test airfield at Brooklands by Sopwith test pilot Harry Hawker, who dazzled onlookers by looping the aircraft three minutes after takeoff. The triplane was very agile, with effective, well-harmonized controls, and did not lose altitude in a turn. Due to the high aspect of the three wings, an observer commented that the aircraft looked like "a drunken flight of steps" when rolling.

The fuselage featured the standard spruce box-girder construction that was braced with wire and hardened with turnbuckles. The forward ends of the longerons were fastened to a fabricated steel spider-band plate that accepted the engine. The very aftermost ends of the longerons terminated in another steel vertical strut fitting that formed the basis for the rudder, variable incidence horizontal stabilizer, and tail skid. The large spruce struts that support the upper plane and middle plane were tied into the framing of the fuselage, being fastened to the two longerons by sturdy metal fittings. The struts were lightened in between the longerons to save on weight, and they terminated at the bottom at the lowermost wing spars; also the aft legs of the landing gear

V-struts had fittings tied into the forward edge of the cabanes. Two arched tube steel cross pieces supported the single Vickers gun at the breech, the aftermost steel former being just aft of the trailing edge of the strut. The struts were joined to the

The Sopwith triplane replica N6290 Dixie II (G-BOCK) of The Shuttleworth Collection flying at an airshow.

The Sopwith triplane replica N500 (G-BWRA) flying at the airshow at Duxford.

three wings by means of a short steel compression fitting that captured the wing spars and the support spar in one fitting.

Aside from the narrow chord, the wings were of standard Sopwith construction; two spars with lightening grooves routed out, light spruce ribs, and riblets between the leading edge and the forward spruce spar. Steel compression fittings and anti-drag rigging connected the two spars. There were ailerons on all three wings. The middle plane had a square notch out at the root to allow the pilot to look forward and down easily. Although most of the construction traits were fairly typical for a Sopwith aircraft, the placement and proportions of the various components was where the genius in this design lay. The narrow chord aided maneuverability, for the shift of the center of pressure with changes of incidence was comparatively small; this allowed the use of a shorter fuselage. At the same time, the distribution of the wing area over three main planes kept the wingspan shorter than a biplane which aided in good roll rate. The spacing, chord and stagger of the three planes afforded superb visibility, and the variable incidence tailplane made trimming this aircraft very easy, making for enjoyable flying (compare this to the constant need to keep the stick forward on a Fokker Dr.1 to keep it level!). In terms of negative aspects of the Sopwith triplane, they were difficult to repair (the fuel and oil tanks were inaccessible without taking the plane apart), and the triplanes required even minor repairs to be executed by rear echelon repair depots. Compounding the frustrations, spare parts became scarce during the summer of 1917, as Sopwith was tooling up for production of the Sopwith Camel. Moreover, the wings of some Clayton & Shuttleworth-built triplanes collapsed in steep dives due to bracing wire that was too weak, which accelerated its obsolescence, and like the Pup, the "Tripehound" also suffered from the single-gun armament at a time when most German fighters had two.[248]

Replica of Raymond Collishaw's Sopwith triplane replica N533 "Black Maria" (ZK-SOP) in New Zealand.

In July 1916, N500 was sent to Dunkirk for evaluation with "A" Naval Squadron, 1 Naval Wing, and was in action within 15 minutes of its arrival. It won instant approval among pilots. The Admiralty and War office were equally enthusiastic, ordering triplanes for both the RNAS and the RFC, to be produced by Sopwith, Clayton & Shuttleworth, and Oakley & Co. The second prototype, serial N504, was fitted with a 130 hp Clerget 9B. N504 first flew on August 26, 1916. With this engine, the triplane could climb 1,000 feet/minute right up to 13,000 feet.[249]

By August and September 1916, Albatros D.1 and D. II aircraft appeared at the front, posing a real threat to the Allied air superiority.[250] This prompted the sending of N504 to the front by November. At this time, the RFC was struggling to ascertain what their premier fighter would be, the triplane or the fast and rugged Spad VII; they opted for the latter relinquishing their orders for triplanes to the RNAS. This is why only this branch was equipped with Sopwith triplanes during the war. This also foreshadowed the direction in aircraft design for the rest of the war: speed. On the Western Front, RNAS triplanes were flown by Squadrons 1, 8, 9, 10, 11 and 12.

Triplane squadrons were gradually replaced with Camels between mid-July to mid-August 1917, and by the end of August, 10 Squadron followed suit. Although only 147 triplanes were built, they had quite an impact on German aircraft design. Many triplanes and quadruplanes were built by top German and Austro-Hungarian aircraft manufacturers in an effort to match or exceed the performance of the Sopwith Triplane. This phenomenon distracted the leadership and aircraft industry long enough to delay focus on the future path of combat aircraft: speed, stable gun platform, and group tactics.

The Sopwith Camel replica D1851 "Ikanopit" photographed by Darren Harbar.

In Profile
Sopwith F.1 Camel

Sopwith F.1 Camel: (B7190) Flt Lt. W. G. R. Hinchliffe, No. 10 (N) Squadron, RNAS; Teteghem, France; March 1918.

The Camel

The most iconic of the Sopwith fighters—the Camel—appeared on December 22, 1916.[251] It was reputed for its hard right turn and twin rapid-firing Vickers machine guns synchronized to fire through the propeller. By grouping all the weight on the CofG up front (guns, pilot, fuel, engine) combined with the gyroscopic effect of the rotary, enabled the Camel to make a very hard and fast right turn—which could also result in a spin rather quickly if the pilot wasn't paying attention (this could also be useful in combat by the experienced pilot). Some 5,747 were built (all types) and were responsible for shooting down some 2,700 German aircraft. Most Camels were built by subcontractors—Ruston Proctor was just one of them.[252] From the first general arrangement to prototype it took just six weeks and became operational within nine months. The Camel was a hard-hitting machine; it had a Hazleton attachment that allowed its rate of fire to be 1,000 rounds/minute.[253]

The Camel owed its lineage to the Pup and triplane, as it had many similarities, but it also had important differences. The empennage was similar to the Pup as was the fuselage aft of the cockpit; forward of the cockpit (seven feet) was very different as all the heavy items—fuel, guns, pilot, ammo, oil, and engine—were grouped tightly together and represented around 90 percent of the total aircraft weight. The wings followed the pattern used by the French Nieuports and by extension the Albatros D.III, D.V, and D.Va; all had little dihedral on the top plane and a modest amount of dihedral on the lower plane. The Camel's lower wing dihedral was pronounced—170° with 178° on the top plane, and 2° of incidence on the top plane at the center section and 3° at the tips; forming slight washout; the lower plane had a uniform incidence of 3°.[254] J. M. Bruce stated that Fred Sigrist wanted the upper plane flat to ease production problems.[255] Like the triplane and Pup, there were ailerons

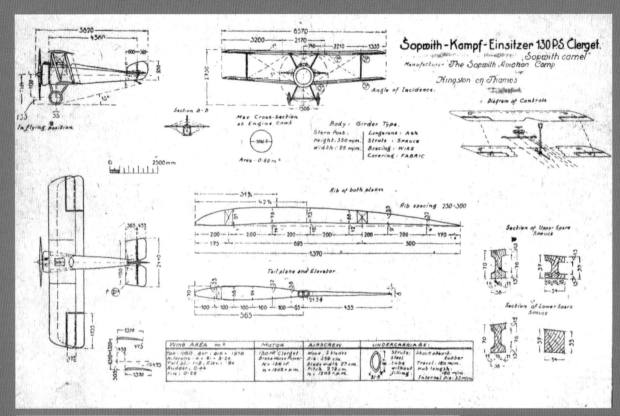

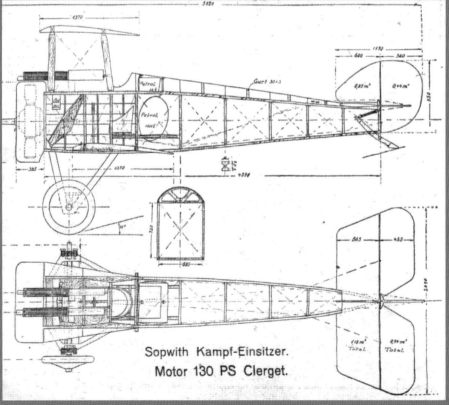

Above, a drawing of the Camel from *Flugsport*. (*Flight*, September 12, 1918)

The Sopwith Camel. (*Flight*, September 12, 1918)

John Shaw: Building the Sopwith Camel

John Shaw was interested in flying from an early age when his father took him for a glider flight in 1958 in a vintage open cockpit glider—after that, he was hooked. He joined the ATC at 14 and they sent him on a gliding course in 1964 when he soloed and was asked to stay on as a staff cadet—a fantastic opportunity for a 16-year-old. He received his pilot's license in 1973 and continued his gliding again. In 1989, he joined the Cornish gliding and flying club with his wife, and continued until about 2005 when the club folded. During that time, both became instructors and John ended up being CFI for over 10 years and technical officer and inspector for even longer. He maintained all the club gliders, and restored many insurance write-offs which were not economically viable as commercial aircraft. His own 83-year-old Tiger Moth was bought in pieces and he spent eight years restoring it to flying condition—completing it in 2005. Due to the CAA making them "orphan aircraft," he moved the Tiger and another aircraft to France where he and his wife went gliding every year. John had a good relationship with the airfield owner, who was also interested in vintage aircraft and he suggested building a vintage aircraft. John decided on the Camel and started work in 2008, getting his certificate to fly it in 2018. The WWI Camel was chosen because it was wood and fabric and known as the Spitfire of WWI, and he could "probably just afford it." The Camel had a bad reputation in WWI as it killed more pilots in training than in actual combat. John cannot tell you a lot about flying it as he had a very short time in the seat due to a mishap, but one of the worst problems with the Camel was/is engine management.

on both wings. The wings were spaced 4.3 feet at the tips, and just under 5 feet at the fuselage, and were joined by solid spruce streamlined interplane struts that were capped on either end by steel cups that were welded to the fittings on the wing spars.[256] The wings were made up of spruce ribs and spars—all being spindled out to form an "I" section, except for the lower aft spar which was left solid.[257]

The Camel's fuselage structure followed that of the Pup and triplane; box-girder, wire-and-turnbuckle-braced construction. As with the Pup and triplane, a fabricated steel spider band capped the front of the longerons to which the 130 hp Clerget engine was mounted. The 36.5-gallon fuel tank and eight-gallon gravity tank were fabricated in some Camels of welded sheet aluminum; in others lead-coated riveted sheet iron.[258] The horizontal stabilizer of symmetrical airfoil was not adjustable like the triplane and some of the Pups, and was fixed at 1.5°.[259] The cockpit was simple and utilitarian but included sufficient instrumentation (like many British aircraft of this period): a manometer (with safety valve), clock, pressure gauge, altimeter, compass, tachometer, pulsometer, and two magneto switches.[260]

There were potentially four prototypes being developed as what J. M. Bruce describes as a "private venture" within the company. Two prototypes ordered separately by the Admiralty (N517 and N518) with the former being tested at Brooklands on February 26, 1917.[261]

Sopwith noted that his other aircraft had a more intuitive/aesthetic approach to their design whereas the Camel featured a more scientific approach:

John Shaw's replica Sopwith Camel fuselage on the side panel building jig. (John Shaw)

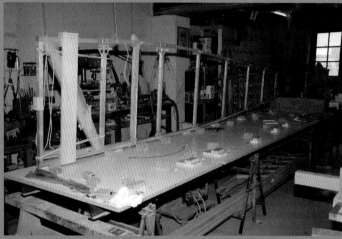

The fuselage panel freed from the building jig and standing upright. (John Shaw)

Both side panels have been built and are erected, plumbed, and aligned along a centerline. (John Shaw)

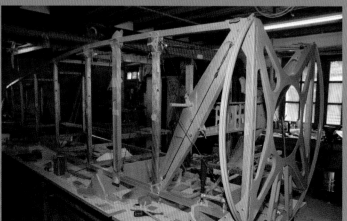

The cross pieces are fitted, as is spider band for mounting the engine. (John Shaw)

A wicker seat with leather cushion has been installed as has the fuel tank. (John Shaw)

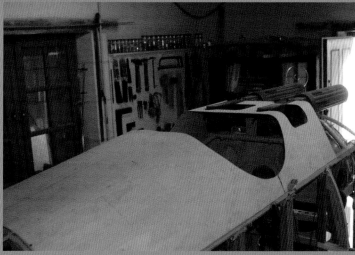

Plywood turtle decking forming the cockpit opening and partial gun breech. (John Shaw)

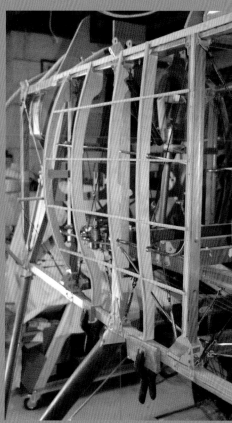

Above, empennage of composite construction; spruce framing of the horizontal stabilizer and steel tube rudder, fin, and elevators. Note the symmetrical airfoil of the horizontal stabilizer. (John Shaw)

Right, plywood formers and spruce stringers forming the transition between the cowling and the slab sides. (John Shaw)

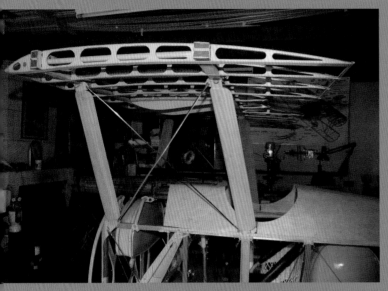

The center section of the Camel to which the cabanes were fastened. This was characteristic of almost all Sopwith aircraft. (John Shaw)

The engine has been fitted to the firewall as have the wheels. (John Shaw)

Striking image of the Camel in the "bones" on a beautiful sunny day. (John Shaw)

The fuselage, empennage, and center section have been covered, doped, and painted. The cheek areas have yet to be covered to allow access to engine and instruments. (John Shaw)

Wing panels have been covered, rib stitched, doped, and painted. Insignia roundels are the finishing touch. (John Shaw)

Left and below, John Shaw's replica/reproduction Camel. (John Shaw)

Camels lined up in the factory awaiting their wings. (Kingston Aviation website, www. kingstonaviation.org)

The 1,000th Camel B7380 produced by Ruston Proctor decorated in an elaborate colorful ancient Egyptian style scheme. (Kingston Aviation website, www. kingstonaviation.org)

All our aeroplanes were built entirely by eye. They weren't stressed at all. The Camel was the product of a more scientific approach. We were just learning how to stress at the time of the Camel. In the hands of a competent pilot, who had made friends with the Camel, it could really play wonderful tricks. But it was a vicious little machine to fly and not easy; and it wasn't everybody's cup of tea. You had to be a good pilot to fly a Camel.[262]

Elliott White Springs, an American fighter pilot who flew Camels with the 148th Aero Squadron, had this to say about them:

A tricky little biplane … they would do about 90 mph level but you couldn't fly level because they would shake your teeth out in forty seconds by the clock. You had to climb or glide. But they could fly upside down and turn inside a stairwell. They would stall at 15,000 feet and lose 1,000 feet in a turn. But they were deadly below 5,000 feet if you could suck the Fokkers down to that level.[263]

… We picked up the castoff rebuilt Camels from Aire. No new Camels had been built since January [1918] when they became obsolete and were replaced by SEs, Dolphins, Bentleys, and Snipes. But that summer they were still the workhorses below 15,000 feet. Camel … [was at a]disadvantage … where speed and height were paramount, but in a dogfight down low nothing could get away from it … a Camel could make a monkey out of an SE or a Fokker at treetop level but it couldn't zoom and it couldn't dive. The Dolphin was worthless because the motors were too unreliable and the Bentleys [engines] and Snipes didn't get to the front until too late.[264]

Shuttleworth's Camel Sopwith Camel F.1 replica D1851 "Ikanopit" on a low-level fly-by.

Above, the modified framing of a two-seater training Camel. This was done in an effort to reduce training accidents and resultant deaths. (Kingston Aviation website, www.kingstonaviation.org)

An instructor pilot and trainee seated in the new "Training Camel." (Kingston Aviation website, www.kingstonaviation.org)

Just like the French Nieuports, the Camel's nose climbed in a left turn, and when you turned right it dove. Arthur Harris, future Marshal of the RAF had this to say: "If you wanted to go into a left turn you put on full right rudder, and if you let go of the stick it looped!"[265]

The Camel in the right hands was a formidable weapon; to the inexperienced or uninitiated, it was unforgiving. Training deaths (380) almost equaled combat deaths (420) such that training, as quickly and efficiently as possible, became paramount. This led to the realization that if students could somehow learn the Camel with an experienced instructor in the same aircraft, these deaths could be significantly reduced. In his *Recollections of an Airman,* Lt. Col. L. A. Strange, who served with the Central Flying School, wrote: "In spite of the care we took, Camels continually spun down out of control when flown by pupils on their solos. At length, with the assistance of Lt. Morgan, who managed our workshops, I took the main tank out of several Camels and replaced [them] with a smaller one, which enabled us to fit in [a] dual control."

To compensate for the added weight of a second person, the guns were removed and the fuel and oil tanks were combined into one, reduced in size, and repositioned just aft of the firewall—training flights lasted under 30 minutes usually, thus a larger capacity tank was not needed. The fatal problem with neophyte Camel pilots centered around a smooth transition between a rich mixture, needed for takeoff, transitioning to a progressively leaner mixture with increased altitude. Too often, the new pilot would not lean out the mixture at the correct time resulting in a stalled engine at low altitude which usually resulted in a bad or fatal crash. The "Training Camel," as it came to be called, was distributed to all the major flying schools and significantly helped in reducing training accidents.

The Dolphin

The triplane and Camel each had excellent visibility for the pilot due to careful and artful placement of the cockpit relative to the spacing, stagger, and placement of the wing panels. The Sopwith Hippo was a nominally successful two-seater that employed reverse staggered wings to afford the pilot unlimited forward, upward, and 360° visibility. It seems plausible that inspiration for the reverse stagger was taken from the D.H.5. The Hippo had a rotary engine, the bulkiness of which was criticized as giving poor visibility. The other plane that contributed to the design path of the Dolphin was the FR.2 which, like the Dolphin, had a deep frontal radiator, and rudder and fin similar to the Camel—Bruce notes that all three of these planes were being developed concurrently, with the Dolphin likely preceding the Hippo.[266] Sopwith must also have been cognizant of how the Hispano-Suiza 200 hp 8B was used both in the Royal Aircraft Factory S.E.5a, and the Spad series of aircraft. Using an inline engine was a new thing for the Sopwith team, so figuring out how to fit everything around it, cool it, and fuel it was a bit problematic with the Dolphin. It was also clear by this time that reaching high altitudes and speed were key factors in a successful fighter.

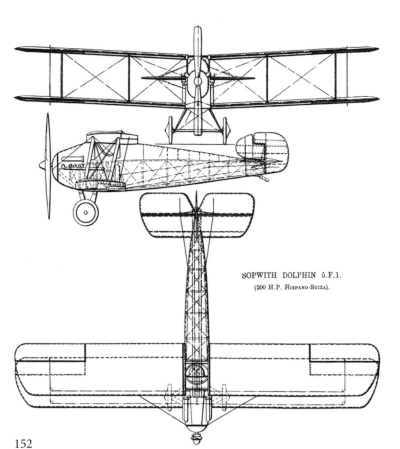

SOPWITH DOLPHIN 5.F.1.
(200 H.P. Hispano-Suiza).

A three-view drawing showing the general arrangement of the Dolphin 5F.1.

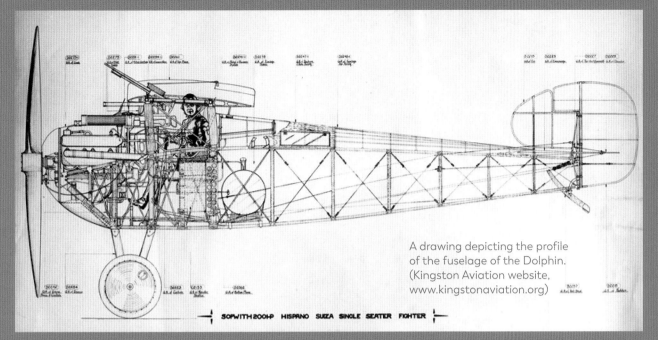

A drawing depicting the profile of the fuselage of the Dolphin. (Kingston Aviation website, www.kingstonaviation.org)

SOPWITH 200HP HISPANO SUIZA SINGLE SEATER FIGHTER

The building jig for the side panels of the Dolphin fuselage. Note how the table itself is set on sawhorses, with a second table top that has been shimmed to dead level with no twist as the floor of the factory was likely not so. Also note the stacks of strut stock and bundles of rigging on the bench. (Kingston Aviation website, www.kingstonaviation.org)

The fuselage erecting jig for the Dolphin—the two control points have been braced athwart as well as fore and aft, and are at the correct heights to make working around the framing efficient. Note how some cross pieces have been fitted in their steel fittings, others wait atop the longerons. On the floor are scraps of wire trimmings. In the distance a control booth with clipboards indicating the progress of the various fuselages. (Kingston Aviation website, www.kingstonaviation.org)

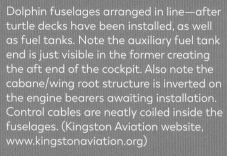

Dolphin fuselages arranged in line—after turtle decks have been installed, as well as fuel tanks. Note the auxiliary fuel tank end is just visible in the former creating the aft end of the cockpit. Also note the cabane/wing root structure is inverted on the engine bearers awaiting installation. Control cables are neatly coiled inside the fuselages. (Kingston Aviation website, www.kingstonaviation.org)

Dolphin Mk I under construction at the Michael Beetham Conservation Centre, which is part of the Royal Air Force Museum Cosford, showing the reverse curve of the upper longeron to advantage—just like a bridge, Sopwith had realized that a reverse curve with its apex at the center was stronger than merely a straight line. Also note the wicker seat positioned up high, and the main fuel tank.

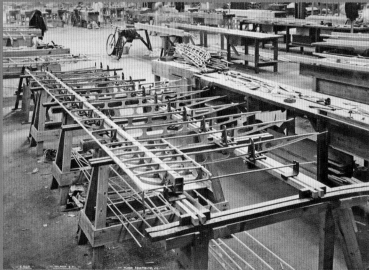

The building jig for the wing panels of the Dolphin. Note the grooved stringers beneath the wing spars; these had adjustable L-shaped brackets that aided in aligning the rib webs relative to the spars. On the next table over, stacks of rib webs await installation. By this time, full-depth riblets had replaced the simple arches of earlier designs. (Kingston Aviation website, www. kingstonaviation.org)

Dolphins under construction—note how they are placed alternately nose facing right then left, then right again to save space in the factory. There also appears to be a fully equipped bench for each airplane. (Kingston Aviation website, www.kingstonaviation.org)

In Profile
Sopwith 5F.1

Sopwith 5F.1 Dolphin: Capt. C. V. Gardner, No.
19 Squadron, RAF; Savy, France; August 1918.

RONNY
BAR
ronnybarprofiles@gmail.com

Thus, the Dolphin's wingspan was increased relative to other Sopwith fighters, to provide sufficient lift at higher altitudes.

The construction of the Dolphin followed typical Sopwith/British practices of a box-girder, wire-and-turnbuckle-braced fuselage, although it was deeper than the Camel providing greater protection for the pilot (head down!). The upper plane attachment system was different in that it was formed by a steel tube cage to which the cabanes and upper wing roots were attached.

The first prototype of the Dolphin was passed through the Experimental Department on May 23, 1917, and its most prominent features were the 13 inches of negative stagger to the wings and the very deep nose radiator, and it was powered by the 150 hp 8B geared Hispano-Suiza. As mentioned, the steel cage that secured the upper wings was also the aperture through which the pilot's head protruded. This arrangement was a bit disconcerting for the novice Dolphin pilot, as he could not see the front of the cowling and thus had a tough time intuitively keeping the plane level as he couldn't line it up with the horizon. The first prototype also had the vertical fin and rudder similar to the Camel, and also like the Camel, Smith grouped all the heavy components together in the nose, hoping to provide the same quick maneuverability that the Camel had but with a very different type of airplane. The twin Vickers guns were mounted directly over the engine, and the pilot sat directly behind the engine with his feet on the rudder bar directly underneath the rear of the crankcase. The 20-gallon main tank was under the seat, with the gravity tank just aft of that. Initially, cooling was provided by two undersized radiators that were fitted under the upper plane wing root near the aft cabane. Due to the radiators being close to the pilot, the hot coolant from the engine kept the cockpit warm and comfortable—this was especially important when flying at higher altitudes. Tweaks with final design were worked out over the three prototypes—the biggest being the final configuration/shape of the cowling, and the positioning of the radiators which ultimately were placed just aft of the pilot. Also, since the pilot's head protruded above the highest point of the aircraft (the upper

Above, Cole Palen, third from left, stands with his band of WWI enthusiasts and restorers in front of his Dolphin in the "bones" in Florida. (Image courtesy of Old Rhinebeck Aerodrome)

Cole's 5F.1 Dolphin N47166 replica today at the Old Rhinebeck Aerodrome—this aircraft is currently being restored to flight-worthy condition. Visible is the Hispano-Suiza "Hisso" engine and slung beneath it is the oil tank. (Image courtesy of Old Rhinebeck Aerodrome)

planes), if it flipped the pilot was in grave danger of breaking his neck. A single/twin Lewis gun "rollbar" was fitted to the third prototype, in subsequent others a semi-circular skid was fitted above the inboard pair of interplanes to afford the pilot at least some protection if the plane ended up inverted. These fears provided largely unfounded with the hoops being retained only in trainers and for the home defense. The first prototype did not have good rudder authority so this was gradually corrected over the next two prototypes.

The only Dolphin that is still flying is currently in the final phases of restoration at the Old Rhinebeck Aerodrome (ORA) in Rhinebeck, New York. According to Tom Polapink of ORA:

This Dolphin was built by Cole Palen, Andy Keefe and several of Cole's helpers in Florida. Cole had a Hispano-Suiza engine and he wanted to build an airplane around it for his air shows at the Old Rhinebeck Aerodrome in NY. He asked his friend Andy Keefe to review original drawings that Cole had of the S.E.5a and the Dolphin to see which would be the better of

Old Rhinebeck Aerodrome's Dolphin in the 1970s when it was flown as a regular part of the airshows held there. (Image courtesy of Old Rhinebeck Aerodrome)

Old Rhinebeck Aerodrome's Dolphin replica today; almost ready to take to the air again. (Image courtesy of Old Rhinebeck Aerodrome)

Cole flying Old Rhinebeck Aerodrome's Dolphin in the 1970s. (Image courtesy of Old Rhinebeck Aerodrome)

The distinctive feature about the Dolphin was the reverse stagger to the wings (13") which is clearly visible in this image.

the two to construct. It turned out that Cole's Dolphin drawing set was more complete than his set of S.E.5a drawings, so he chose to build the Dolphin.

It was completed in 1977 and flew at Old Rhinebeck up until 1990. It was a reliable performer for the most part. One fall day during a show, the engine quit while over the trees and pilot Dick King was unable to make it back to the runway for an emergency landing. The aircraft was heavily damaged, but Dick walked away with minor cuts and bruises.

Repairs began not too long after the crash, but work on the Dolphin was sporadic and was done over many years by many different people. One mechanic who worked on the project in the early 2000s was Bill Gordon. Bill was probably best known for being part of the "Iron Eagles" aerobatic team, and he flew in many major airshows over the years. His grandfather, William F. Gordon, flew Dolphins during World War I, so plans were made to replicate the aircraft that his grandfather was thought to have flown. A photo exists of William F. Gordon and his squadron mates for the No.19 squadron seated beside a Dolphin with a big "G" on the side of the fuselage. This aircraft was used primarily by Captain V.C. Gardner, but he was also known to let other pilots fly it occasionally. It is not known specifically which Dolphin Gordon was most associated with during the war, but the existence of this photo with him beside a Dolphin from his squadron carrying a "G" on the fuselage made it a good candidate, so this is the one that was selected. Sadly, Aerodrome mechanic Bill Gordon perished while ditching a P-47 Thunderbolt in the Hudson River in 2016, during a photo-shoot. The engine failed and Bill did a miraculous job of gently putting it down in the water with minimal damage to the aircraft, but he was unable to escape from the cockpit as the heavy aircraft sunk. Plans are to continue to finish the Dolphin as "G" from the No. 19 squadron in tribute to William F. Gordon and his grandson Bill.

Ken Cassens and Mark Mondello have made the latest push to complete the repair/restoration and did quite a bit of work to iron out some of the problems that arose as a result of so many different people working on it over a long span of time. Ken rebuilt the nose forward of the cockpit and made a new sub-wing. The controls were freed up and the fuselage turnbuckles were adjusted to straighten out the fuselage. The wing structures were varnished by a group of volunteers during a varnishing work party, and final repairs, covering and painting of the wings was done by Karl Erickson of Maine. Jim Millinchuk of New Hampshire is building all new interplane and cabane struts, and all new flying and landing wires will be made up as well. The engine was sent out for overhaul to John Gaertner of Blue Swallow Aircraft in Virginia and it is hoped to have the Dolphin completed in the next year or two.

In speaking with Mark Mondello, he mentioned that the Dolphin was a complicated aircraft around the cockpit and engine compartment due to the extremely close fit of all the components.

Humber Ltd. Bentley B.R.2 engine. (National Air and Space Museum)

The Snipe

Although it did not arrive on the front until late August 1918, the Snipe still deserves mention as it was an excellent fighter that was developed during the war. J. M. Bruce noted that the Snipe "was a small, compact, single-bay biplane in which considerable trouble had been taken to give the pilot a better view than he had on the Camel, yet without resorting to the radical layout of the Dolphin."[267] The Snipe had a deep fuselage, and the pilot sat at a strategic location so that he could see over the top wing yet not be so exposed as in the Dolphin. Like the Dolphin, it had long wings with equal dihedral on both and the tail borrowed from its predecessors, with the rudder being very similar to the Camel on early

Snipe prototype B9965 with fully rounded and faired fuselage, although still single bay. Note the port interplane mounted airspeed indicator, and the two crescent-shaped footholds needed to ascend to the high cockpit. (Kingston Aviation website, www.kingstonaviation.org)

models. Unlike the Camel, it would prove easier to fly (thus easier on green pilots), had a better rate of climb and high-altitude performance. It could do 7 mph faster than the Camel's 115 mph at 10,000 feet and it had fuel tanks large enough for three hours of flight time.

Staying true to good production practices, the Snipe was designed to utilize engines already employed in the Camel, such the 150 hp B.R.1, 150 hp Gnome Monosoupape, 130 hp Clerget 9B or 110 hp Le Rhône.[268] The first prototype had a 150 hp B.R.I engine, and was test flown during the summer of 1917. As a result of this test and given the company's excellent track record, Sopwith was commissioned to produce six prototypes: B9962–B9967. Walter O. Bentley designed the B.R.2 engine concurrently with the B.R.I but had to wait until the 150 hp engine proved itself satisfactory before authority was given for prototype B.R.2 engines to be made.

The construction of the Snipe was not dissimilar from other Sopwith aircraft, in that by this time Sopwith had a proven production methodology. The standard box-girder fuselage was at the core of the streamlined fuselage, with plywood formers fastened to the vertical spruce struts, and then stringers fitted into notches in these. The wings followed suit with some of the French aircraft like the Spads, in that plywood sheathed the riblet area of the leading edge. The horizontal stabilizer was adjustable, as one drawback to the Camel had been that since there was no adjustment to the tailplane, the pilot had to keep the stick forward to keep the aircraft level.

View of Shuttleworth's Snipe showing guns, cockpit, and various other details. Beneath the formers and fairings, the basic box-girder, wire-braced structure is visible that was characteristic on all Sopwith aircraft. (Kingston Aviation website, www. kingstonaviation.org)

SOPWITH "SNIPE" 7.F.I/5. – 200 H.P. BENTLEY ROTARY ENGINE. – MARCH 11/18.

Snipe showing cheek cowling and fabric covering the details in the previous image. Note how strategically the center section is placed; just low enough to allow the pilot to see over the wing, and just high enough to allow accurate sighting of the gun. (Kingston Aviation website, www. kingstonaviation.org)

Far left, a replica Snipe built by The Vintage Aviator Ltd. in New Zealand.

A close-up of The Vintage Aviator Ltd.'s Snipe F2367 replica showing the harmonious placement of engine (B.R.2), twin Vickers, and cutout in the upper plane to allow the pilot excellent visibility.

Snipes and Salamanders being built in quantity at the factory in Ham in December 1918. (Kingston Aviation website, www.kingstonaviation.org)

The next Snipe prototype (B9963) featured a B.R.2 engine—this would be the last time the RAF ordered an aircraft with a rotary engine. Bruce commented that this next prototype was so similar to the B.R.1 prototype that it may have been a modification of the first one, arriving at Farnborough on November 23, 1917.[269] Performance improved with the more powerful engine but the greater torque made it pull to the right. The rudder which was nominally effective on the Camel proved unwieldy on the B.R.2.[270]

The next prototype featured a reconfigured vertical fin and rudder, and the fuselage and wings were also modified. For example, the single-bay wings were retained but the center section was widened; this meant that the centersection struts flared outward as in the Camel and Pup instead of being vertical as on the original B.R.I and B.R.2 aircraft. The upper wing panels were correspondingly shortened in span and the cut-out in the center section was considerably smaller than the corresponding aperture on the earlier version of the design. The aerodynamic form of the fuselage was improved by fairing the sides; the stringers ran back as far as the penultimate vertical spacer on each side. This modification enhanced the appearance and performance of the aircraft and probably improved the airflow over the tail surfaces. The underside of the fuselage remained flat. An enlarged horn-balanced rudder was fitted, together with an unusually small fin of very low aspect ratio.

The Snipe competed against three other B.R.2-powered fighter prototypes—the Austin Osprey triplane, the Boulton & Paul Bobolink and the Nieuport B.N.1. All three aircraft performed reasonably well and were close in performance data. However, due to Sopwith's excellent reputation, track record, and quality, the Snipe was chosen for a production run of 1,700 aircraft in March 1918.

In 1918, 4,500 Snipes were ordered, with production ending in 1919. With just under 500 being built, the remainder of the contract was cancelled due to the war's conclusion. In addition to the parent company, Snipes were built under license by Boulton & Paul Ltd, Coventry Ordnance Works, D. Napier & Son, Nieuport and Ruston Proctor—much in the way Camels were produced.

The Vintage Aviator Ltd's Snipe F2367 replica in flight.

This engine, a RR Falcon III, is similar to the Falcon I that powered the "Brisfit" fighter (F.2b).

Engines and Props

The following is a brief overview of some of the powerplants and propeller manufacturing methods that were used in British aircraft during the war. In terms of engines, Britain followed France and Germany in their progression from rotaries to inline engines, and used many of the same powerplants as France, but also developed some superb engines that were distinctly British. Propellers began as a one-off, handcrafted piece of precision woodwork that with the advent of duplicating machines, became production oriented—the same was true with various struts, spars, etc. Tire manufacture was a separate animal, and is not discussed in this book.

80 hp Le Rhône 9C

The 80 hp Le Rhône was the workhorse rotary engine for the Sopwith Pup, Camel, Avro 504, D. H. 5, and many French aircraft. Of the Le Rhône engines it was perhaps the sweetest of the lot, having few problems and an excellent power-to-weight ratio. Although rated at 80 hp it was capable of 93 hp at 1,200 rpm. It was fitted with a double thrust ball race, which meant it could be used either in a pusher or tractor configuration. The engine had nine cylinders which were fitted with cast iron liners, and no obturator rings were fitted. The cylinders were threaded into the crankcase. The engine worked on the 4-stroke cycle; two revolutions of the engine yielding one cycle (four strokes in each cylinder). It had nine curving copper induction pipes which allowed the fuel/air mixture from the crankcase to the inlet valves. The engine rotated counterclockwise as seen from the propeller. The engine used approximately one gallon of castor oil per hour of use, and consumed 6–7 gallons of gas (petrol) per hour and it weighed 240 lbs.

The crankshaft was of chrome nickel steel and was hollow and stationary. It was the mounting point for the engine (the engine spun around it), and conveyed oil to the working parts of the engine, and the carburetor was mounted to the rear of this shaft which acted as an induction pipe. It provided (in the crankpin) the fixed point against which the force of the explosion exerted itself in turning the engine, and by extension, the propeller.

The 80 hp Le Rhône Model 9C rotary engine. Note the copper induction pipes on the face of the 80 hp model; a sure way to differentiate it from its 110 hp brother.

The 80 hp Le Rhône were built by the Union Switch and Signal co. in Swissvale, PA, U.S., under license. Pictured here is the final weighing and assembly of cylinders. (U.S. National Archives)

A picture of the boring of the cylinder bosses in the crankcase. Note the blank awaiting boring on the floor to the left. (U.S. National Archives)

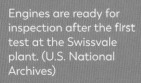

Engines are ready for inspection after the first test at the Swissvale plant. (U.S. National Archives)

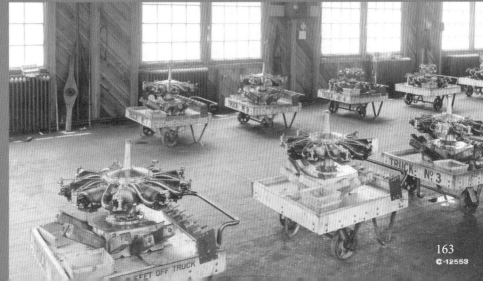

163

Tony Wytenburg: Re-manufacturing Engines

One of CAMS Gnome rotaries on the test stand.

Tony Wytenburg owns Classic Aero Machining Services (CAMS) located on Omaka Airfield in Marlborough, New Zealand. According to Tony, it is a "genuine one-stop service for the reverse engineering and re-manufacture of metal aircraft parts for WWI, WWII, modern and experimental aeroplanes including engines." His Gnome reproduction engines, which include some modern improvements that make them run leaner and cleaner, are particularly interesting. He describes his operation as:

With over 115 years of combined experience in the trade, the small team of 4 machinists/engineers at CAMS have the experience and know-how to tackle any job, big or small.

Using original drawings or reverse engineering from original aircraft parts or engines, replacements are re-manufactured to the highest standards replicating both the performance and appearance of the originals. Production ranges from the smallest brackets to complete engines. With their in-house test rigs and computerized engine dyno, CAMS can provide everything from initial drawings through to performance assessment and verification. Successful re-manufacture of the RAF 1a engine and Gnome 100 hp Monosoupape engine is a testament to the services available.

The CAMS team are not only exceptional craftsmen and engineers, but enthusiasts for their work as well. Nothing gives them more satisfaction than to start with a corroded, badly damaged part, figure out how it worked, redesign it then the critical bit—figuring out how to re-manufacture it. Then down to the workshop and watch as a new part—both functional and beautiful—emerges from a billet of raw metal.

The steel crankcase was made in one piece, and had nine threaded openings to receive the cylinders. It had an extension ring on the propeller side of the engine to accept the tappet guides and induction pipes. The valves on each cylinder were actuated by a single rocker arm that alternately opened/closed the exhaust valve and the intake valve. When the arm moved down it opened the intake valve, and when it moved up it opened the exhaust valve. To make this system work, a two-way push-pull rod was fitted. The Le Rhônes had a total loss oil system; much of which ending up on the airplane and in the pilot's face!

Le Rhône engines were produced by Société des Moteurs Gnome et Rhône, which had bought out Société des Moteurs Le Rhône in January 1914—they were competitors up until this point. The Le Rhône was produced in Germany (by Motorenfabrik Oberursel), Austria, the United Kingdom (by Daimler), Russian Empire and Sweden.

Le Rhône 110 hp 9J

The Le Rhône 9J, appearing in 1916, operated much like the 80 hp, however the induction pipes were fitted to the aft side of the engine, and were round at the crankcase instead of flattened. It was fitted to many aircraft including the Camel, Pup, Strutter, Nieuport 17, Avro 304, D.H.2, D.H.5, Bristol M.1, and the Hanriot HD.1—plus many others. The 9Jb could generate up to 130 hp but these were mainly fitted to French aircraft.

The Le Rhône 110 hp 9J. Note the induction pipes on the aft side of the engine. Although more powerful, the 110 hp was nominally less reliable than the 80 hp model.

A close-up of the Gnome Omega's faceplate.

The Gnome Monosoupape Omega 7 cylinder 80 hp rotary engine exhibited at the Science Musuem, London.

A Gnome B2 on test stand with prop. (U.S. National Archives)

The Gnome Monosoupape 9-cylinder 100 hp type B2.

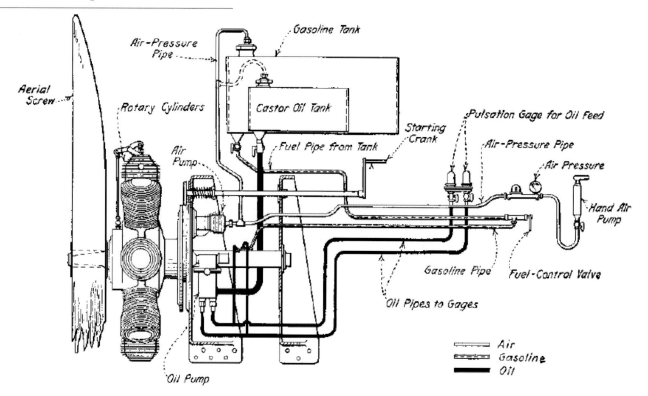

A diagram showing the travel and supply of gas, oil, and air to the B2 Gnome engine.

Gnome Monosoupape 80 hp 7-cylinder Type A

The Gnome engines operated differently from the Le Rhône in that the fuel induction occurred in the piston head, with exhaust expelled from the cylinder head. The 80 hp version was used in the early Pups and Avro 504s. It had seven machined nickel steel cylinders and could deliver 65 hp even though it was rated for 80 hp. It had a double-thrust ball race which, like its Le Rhône counterpart, could be used in either a tractor or pusher, and was also a 4-stroke. One of the things that made it very different from the Le Rhône was that it had automatic fuel inlet valves that were situated in the piston heads.

The Gnome 7-cylinder consumed 1.5 to 1.75 gallons of oil per hour, and used 7–8 gallons of fuel per hour. The engine weight 210 lbs., and was made chiefly of steel. Like the Le Rhône, it had a nickel steel crankshaft, and functioned much in the same way. The crankcase was made from two steel stampings fastened together by steel bolts, and the cylinders were firmly attached to two parts of the crankcase and were prevented from turning by means of a key. The pistons were made from cast iron, and the heads were bored to receive the fuel inlet valve. The piston arms were hollow to allow the fuel mixture to travel to the head. The bronze carburetor was located on the aft end of the hollow

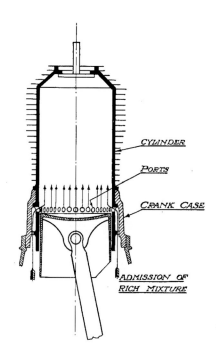

A drawing illustrating the fuel intake of a Gnome Monosoupape cylinder.

The Gnome 9 Delta on display at the Musée des Arts et Métiers, Paris.

crankshaft, and included an air intake and fuel needle valve which controlled the fuel/air mixture. The engine was lubricated by means of an oil pump, providing pressure, and centrifugal force which drew the oil/ gas air mixture to the extremities of the spinning engine. Castor oil was used as it did not break down as quickly as other oils when mixed with fuel. Lubrication traveled to the various parts of the engine by means of passageways let into the crankcase. As with all rotaries, the oil system was a total-loss type (it was not recycled).

Gnome Monosoupape 100 hp 9 cylinder, Type B-2

The Gnome 9 cylinder B-2, appearing in 1917, was a very popular engine in that it was fitted to the D.H.2, D.H.5, Avro 504, Bristol Scout, the Sopwith Pup, F.1 Camel, and Vickers "Gunbus." It operated much like the Gnome 7 cylinder, only with more power due to the increase in cylinders. It could develop 100 hp at 1,200 rpm and weighed 272 lbs.

Gnome Monosoupape 160 hp 9 cylinder, Type N

This engine was used on the Camel and Nieuport 28, and operated much in the same way the other Gnomes did, except it generated around 160 hp due to an increased bore and stroke. It had increased torque due to its power, which was both a blessing and curse on the Camel, and was reputed to have high fuel consumption.

The Clerget 130 hp 9B on display at the Fleet Air Arm Museum, Yeovilton.

A period drawing of the Clerget 130 hp 9B.

Clerget 130 hp 9B

This rotary was rated at 110 hp but could develop 130 hp at 1,200 rpm. Like the other engines, it could be used as a pusher or tractor, and it too was a 4-stroke cycle; two revolutions of the engine yielding one cycle (4 strokes). It differed from the Le Rhônes and Gnomes in that it had aluminum alloy pistons. The connecting rods were tubular in section, and the inlet and exhaust cams were operated mechanically by means of separate tappets, arms, and rockers. Aside from the pistons, the rest of the engine was primarily of steel, and rotation was counter-clockwise.

The Clerget 130 hp would typically burn around 2 gallons of castor oil/hour, 10 gallons of petrol/hour, with a total weight of 365 pounds—significantly heavier than the Le Rhônes and Gnomes. The crankshaft was of forged steel, and it was hollow and acted as a conveyance for fuel/air/oil mixture. The crankcase was similar to the Gnomes, in that two steel stamping sandwiched the cylinders between the halves, and then were bolted together; mechanically trapping the cylinders by means of grooves and ridges in cylinder and crankcase at the base.

The cylinders were of nickel steel that were machined from a solid block, yielding walls of 3 mm. Fuel inlet and exhaust apertures were bored into the cylinder head, and the fuel/air/oil mixture was delivered by means of induction tubes mounted to the aft side of the cylinders slightly off-center. The carburetor was mounted horizontally to end of crankshaft and operated similarly to the Gnomes and Le Rhônes. These engines were used on the Sopwith Camel, triplane, Strutter, and the Avro 504, plus many other aircraft.

The Hispano-Suiza 8A 150-200 hp

Swiss engineer Marc Birkigt designed the first cast aluminum engine block for the Hispano-Suiza automobile and engineering company in 1904 which yielded a light and powerful inline engine. In 1914, Birkigt modified the engine for aviation use and it made its appearance in February 1915. The engine was a 90° V-8 engine featuring steel cylinder sleeves fitted to a cast-aluminum engine block with the inlets and exhaust ports as

The Hispano-Suiza 8A 150 hp.

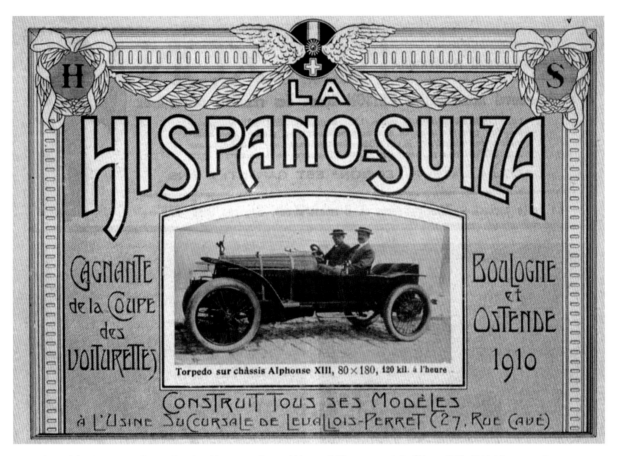

An ad for Hispano-Suiza for the Hispano-Suiza Alfonso XIII automobile (Type 15T), 1911. Hispano-Suiza engines were originally for automobiles.

part of the casting. The crankshaft was milled from a solid block of steel. The valves were actuated by using a bevel gear-driven tower shaft on the aft side of each cylinder bank, that was in turn actuated by the crankshaft. Each cylinder had dual spark plugs for reliability. This engine made the Spad VII possible and eventually the S.E.5a and Sopwith Dolphin. The 8Ab featured an increased compression ratio—from 4.7 to 5.3 giving it 180 hp. In 1918, the Wolseley Viper was created which was a high compression derivative of the "Hisso", generating between 200–210 hp. These were made under license in England at the Wolseley factory.

Bentley B.R.1

This engine was developed by Lt. Walter O. Bentley for the RNAS. It was inspired by the Clerget 9B and also in concept borrowed from the Hisso—it had aluminum cylinders with cast iron sleeves; so not unlike the cast aluminum block and steel sleeves of that engine. It also had aluminum pistons—taking one of the best features of that engine while minimizing its drawbacks which included its expense and susceptibility to overheating. Therefore the idea of using aluminum cylinders in the Bentley (that could absorb heat more readily) made sense. The Bentley also featured (like the Hisso) dual ignition, and a longer stroke thus producing around 150 hp. The engine was first called the A.R.1 (Admiralty Rotary) but was then changed to B.R.1 (Bentley Rotary) and were ordered in large quantities, however, there were never enough to replace the Clerget engines entirely as these continued to be produced under license.

A Humber-built Admiralty AR.1 Bentley B.R.1 displayed at the Militärhistorisches Museum Flugplatz Berlin-Gatow.

The Bentley B.R.2.

Bentley B.R.2

The B.R.2 was developed from the B.R.1 in an effort to increase horsepower, which was successfully increased to 230 hp. It was also 93 pounds heavier than the B.R.1. The B.R.2 was designed specifically for the Sopwith Snipe; neither the Snipe nor the B.R.2 arrived in time to make a decisive difference in the war.

Propellers

When the war began, there were only about 20 propeller makers in England. Beginning in 1916, leadership began recruiting production woodworking firms such as Maple & Co., H.H. Martyn & Co. and White Allom & Co. In an article in *Flight* magazine in 1921, the production of an airscrew was described at the Falcon Airscrew company and is excerpted as follows:

> Stored in the yards are large quantities of mahogany and walnut of the finest quality. These yards are kept well stocked, and the timber is allowed to remain for many months before being used, so as to ensure that it is well seasoned. The seasoned timber is conveyed from the yards to the sawmill and planing shops, in which it is sawn into planks and thicknessed ready for use. From templates carefully prepared the planks are then marked off and sawn to shape, corresponding to their respective laminations.
>
> The next operation is heating preparatory to the glueing down and clamping of the laminations. In front of a huge fire the planks are warmed to the required degree, and are then placed in their proper position in the jigs, glued together, and clamped down. Here they are allowed to remain for 24 hours until the glue has thoroughly set. They are then lifted off the jigs and taken to the shaping shop, where the edges of the laminations are removed nearly down to the joint lines.
>
> In the shaping and finishing shops these roughly-shaped blocks of laminated wood are turned over to highly-skilled craftsmen, who, making lavish use of gauges and templates, reduce the wood further until the actual sizes called for on the drawings are reached. Before reaching the finished size, the propeller has to be repeatedly balanced to see that one blade is not heavier than another. The effect of even quite minute differences in weight would seriously upset the smooth running of the airscrew, and would give rise to vibration. If, then, the craftsman discovers that one blade is heavier than the other, he has to make up his mind, some considerable time before the finished shape is reached, whether the lack of balance is due to the, at that time, more or less rough state of the propeller If he

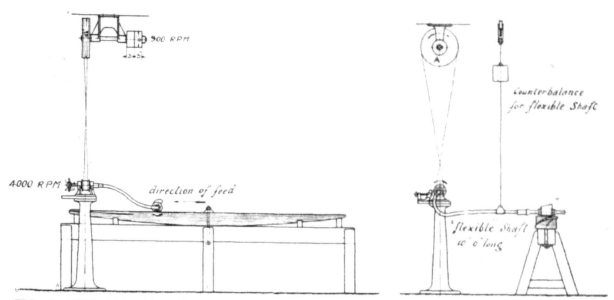

FIG. 5.—SHOWING THE FLEXIBLE SHAFT DRIVE ARRANGEMENT.—The countershaft, A, must be placed directly over the centre of the stand and drive by cross-belt as shown. Belt 1½ ins. wide.

A diagram showing the setup of the Rotary Shaping Machine. (*Flight*, December 14, 1916)

decides that after finishing one blade will still be heavier than the other, he has to leave the lighter blade just a trifle over size. (We believe the Air Ministry allows 1 mm). The other blade is then worked to exact size, and the propeller is put on a sensitive machine, which discloses any difference in balance.

To finish up the propeller is sand-papered [sanded], covered with fabric which is glued on. Then it is painted, and the brass tips are screwed and riveted to the tips and leading edge. This part of the work also calls for great accuracy; as does indeed every operation in the manufacture of an airscrew.[271]

The article notes that during the war, the type of craftsmanship described above had to be supplanted to an extent by machines in the interest of production. The following is from another article from *Flight* outlining the value of what they call a "Rotary Shaping Machine" which appears to be a "flex shaft" mandrel type grinder/sander in the modern sense. The machine was rated at 1 hp in terms of its power, and claimed to be able to rough out a propeller in just two hours vs. one day of doing the same work by hand. The article goes on to say that the machine can be used in any woodworking trade—from furniture to shipbuilding. It was being marketed and manufactured by Messrs. Thomas Robinson and Son.[272] The line of duplicating machines by Wadkin & Co. were designed to copy a master form (be it a prop or strut) from a block of stock to quickly reproduce the shape.

Wadkin & Co's "Automatic Propeller Shaper," a machine that took a master shape (i.e. propeller) and copied it on a blank piece of stock. This type of machine increased production, but there was some loss in quality from the hand-shaped propellers. (*Flight*, July 27, 1916)

| Conclusion

In conclusion, the British aircraft industry per se did not exist before the war. Aircraft were hand-crafted and were usually of a proven design like the Wright Flyer, Farman or Bleriot aircraft—and built under license. Innovation proceeded cautiously and did not have government support initially. The true British pioneers forged ahead anyway, fueled by their passion for flight and caught up in the frenzy over aviation that was occurring in France. When Bleriot crossed the Channel in 1909, the government took another view—led by Lord Northcliffe and others, it was determined that with the advent of airpower, Britain no longer enjoyed projection from her navy or her island status. By the eve of World War One, a few visionaries were producing aircraft such as Tommy Sopwith, A. V. Roe, and others. Moreover, the Royal Aircraft factory had been established, and was meant to be a clearing house for the best information on aircraft design and construction. Also, numerous flying schools were operating to further the cause of aviation as a whole, and to provide income to keep their owners afloat while their aircraft were slowly and painstakingly built. After the war began, the design process was accelerated exponentially—designs that were production-worthy had to be built quickly to uniform standards, so the era of complex hand-crafted machines, like Farmans, Wright Flyers, etc. suddenly became impractical. Add to this limited supplies of wood, which forced designers to design aircraft that could be built well, but using sparing amounts of material. Furthermore, the labor force that was to build these planes did not exist. Men trained as cabinetmakers, boat-builders, instrument-makers, etc. were quickly co-opted to build aircraft; designs for which were often only just percolating in the designer's head.

British designers did not try new construction methods in the way that the Germans did—for example, the use of monocoque construction was limited to various portions of the cowling and turtle deck as opposed to full-blown fuselages like the Albatros, Pfalz, and Roland fighters. The use of welded steel was also limited to empennages, wing tips and various minor structural components; nothing like what was practiced by Fokker. British fuselages tended to favor the tried-and-true box-girder, wired-braced construction, and wing construction of the typical type—spruce spars with ribs slid into place, resulting in robust bracing wires and struts. That being said, British designers pushed the limits of these parameters resulting in iconic designs such as the Sopwith Pup, Camel, Dolphin, the S.E.5a, and the Bristol Fighter. Additional significant innovations included the adaptation of a semi-modern cockpit which included much more instrumentation than either the French or German counterparts.

In terms of the industry as a whole, there was dynamic change—where once there had been no trained aircraft builders, now there was a labor force numbering in the thousands—many of whom were women. British women working in aircraft factories served to not only help build the industry materially, but also underscored nascent aspirations of women's suffrage, work-place equality and a sense of self-worth. In addition, new machinery was developed to increase production such as spar and propeller shapers, and all manner of other ancillary devices that accelerated efficient production and of aircraft parts. After the war ended, some companies folded but others flourished and morphed into businesses that survive today—without the determination, perserverence, and ingenuity of the early British pioneers, aircraft such as the de Havilland Mosquito, and Avro Lancaster & Vulcan, and Hawker Hurricane and Harrier Jump Jet—would never have come to pass.

Appendix 1
The 1915 Defence of the Realm Act

Be it enacted by the King's most Excellent Majesty, by and with the advice and consent of the Lords Spiritual and Temporal, and Commons, in this present Parliament assembled, and by the authority of the same, as follows:

His Majesty in Council has power during the continuance of the present war to issue regulations for securing the public safety and defence of the realm, and as to the powers and duties for that purpose of the Admiralty and Army Council and of the members of His Majesty's forces and other persons acting on his behalf; and may by such regulations authorise the trial by courts-martial, or in the case of minor offences by courts of summary jurisdiction, and punishment of persons committing offences against the regulations and in particular against any of the provisions of such regulations designed …

It shall be lawful for the Admiralty or Army Council—

(a) to require that there shall be placed at their disposal the whole or any part of the output of any factory or workshop in which arms, ammunition, or warlike stores or equipment, or any articles required for the production thereof, are manufactured;

(b) to take possession of and use for the purpose of His Majesty's naval or military service any such factory or workshop or any plant thereof; and regulations und this Act may be made accordingly.

Defence of the Realm Act Catalogue reference: MUN 5/19/221/8, 5 Geo. 5. Defence of the Realm Consolidation Act, 1914, Ch.8. An Act to consolidate and amend the Defence of the Realm Acts. 27th November 1914. http://www.nationalarchives.gov.uk/pathways/firstworldwar/transcripts/first_world_war/defence_ofthe-realm.htm

Appendix 2
Aircraft Designer Patents

A. V. Roe Patents

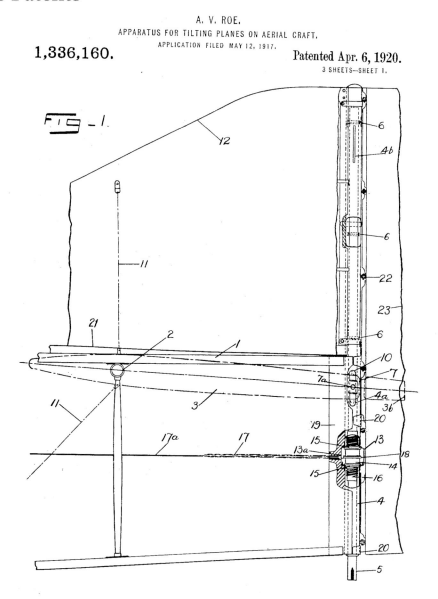

A. V. ROE.
APPARATUS FOR TILTING PLANES ON AERIAL CRAFT.
APPLICATION FILED MAY 12, 1917.

1,336,160.

Patented Apr. 6, 1920.
3 SHEETS—SHEET 1.

A.V. Roe
Inventor
per Geo. A. Hutchinson
Attorney

This mechanism enabled the horizontal stabilizer and elevators to vary the angle of incidence (up or down) to trim the aircraft in flight, thus eliminating the need for the stick to compensate for excessive climbing or diving of the aircraft.

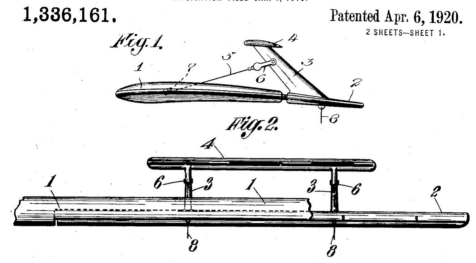

A. V. ROE AND R. J. PARROTT.
STABILIZING PLANE ON AERIAL CRAFT.
APPLICATION FILED JAN. 4, 1919.

1,336,161.

Patented Apr. 6, 1920.

2 SHEETS—SHEET 1.

Fig. 1.

Fig. 2.

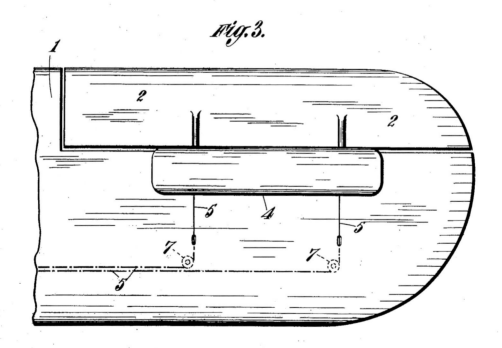

Fig. 3.

This patent was for what amounted to a balancing mechanism for control surfaces, which made them easier to handle from the cockpit (the pilot didn't have to use as much muscle to move various control surface).

INVENTORS
Albert Verdon Roe and
Reginald John Parrott,
By Geo. A. Hutchinson,
attorney.

A. V. ROE.

CONTROLLING GEAR FOR AIRCRAFT.

APPLICATION FILED OCT. 31, 1918.

1,343,850.

Patented June 15, 1920.

6 SHEETS—SHEET 1.

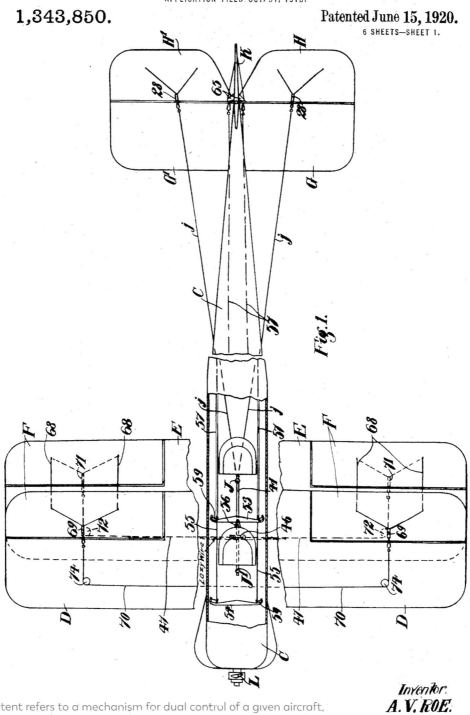

Fig.1.

This patent refers to a mechanism for dual control of a given aircraft, such that tandem cockpits as each are equipped with a full set of controls. This was important for training as well as combat if the pilot was injured/killed the observer could then take control of the airplane.

Inventor.
A. V. ROE.
BY. Eugene C. Brown
Attorney.

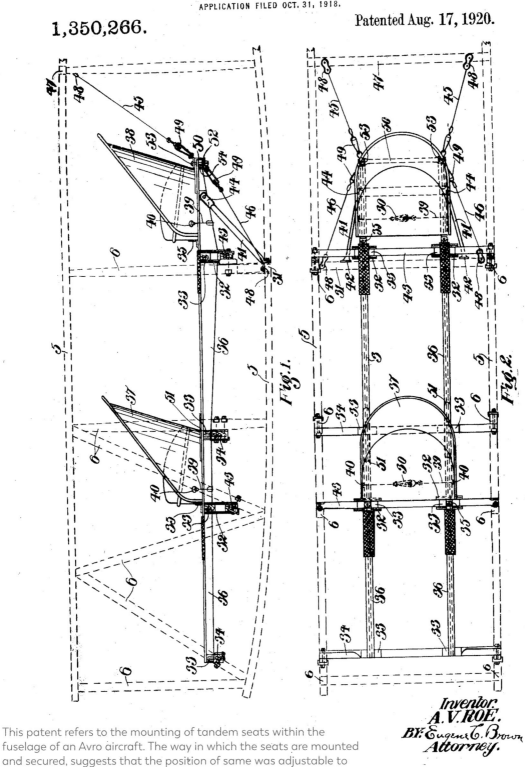

A. V. ROE.
SEAT SUPPORT ON AIRCRAFT.
APPLICATION FILED OCT. 31, 1918.

1,350,266.

Patented Aug. 17, 1920.

This patent refers to the mounting of tandem seats within the fuselage of an Avro aircraft. The way in which the seats are mounted and secured, suggests that the position of same was adjustable to some degree.

A. V. ROE.
MOUNTING FOR GUNS.
APPLICATION FILED DEC. 1, 1917.

1,382,241.

Patented June 21, 1921.
3 SHEETS—SHEET 1.

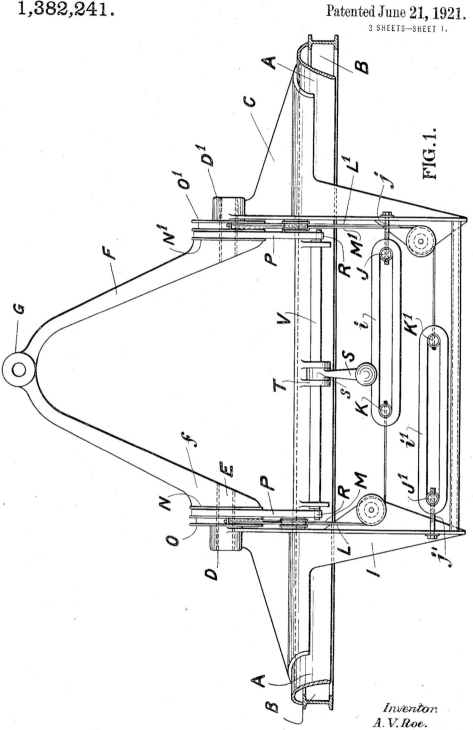

FIG. 1.

Inventor.
A. V. Roe.
per. Geo. A. Hutchinson
Attorney.

This patent describes a gun mounting mechanism that allows a machine gun (Lewis gun) to rotate and elevate using an armature that moves about a fixed ring, that is in turn mounted to the fuselage. This device could also be used aboard ships thus lending greater application/appeal to the invention.

T. Sopwith Patents

T. SOPWITH.

LANDING CHASSIS OR UNDER CARRIAGE OF AEROPLANES AND THE LIKE.

APPLICATION FILED MAY 12, 1917.

1,239,736.

2 Sheets
Sheet No. 1.

Patented Sept. 11, 1917.

2 SHEETS—SHEET 1.

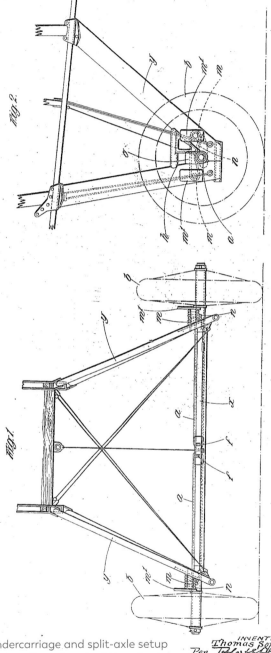

This patent refers to a V-strut undercarriage and split-axle setup for Sopwith aircraft. This mechanism allowed each of the wheels to be setup on bungees independent of one another, such that each wheel responds to bumps in terrain separately (as opposed to a single contiguous axle). Each end of the two axles is hinged on a pin in the middle of the spreader.

INVENTOR:
Thomas Sopwith
Per Robert O. Phillip
Attorney

T. O. M. SOPWITH.
WIND SCREEN FOR USE WITH AIRCRAFT GUNS.
APPLICATION FILED AUG. 14, 1917.

1,249,535.

Patented Dec. 11, 1917.

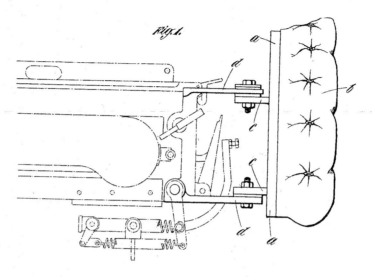

Fig. 1.

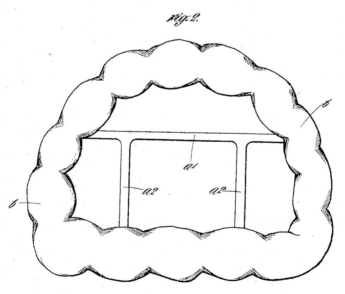

Fig. 2.

INVENTOR.
T. O. M. Sopwith.

Per

Attorney.

This patent describes a padded windscreen that was mounted directly to the rear breech of the Vickers machine gun. It allowed the pilot to sight the gun closely, and protected him against hitting his head on a rough landing or turbulent air.

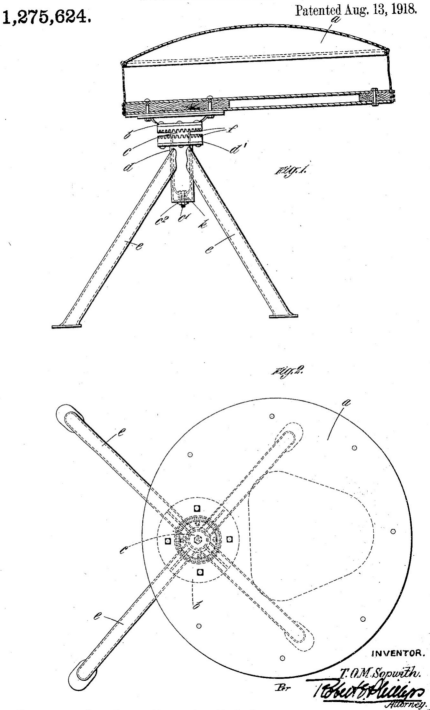

T. O. M. SOPWITH.

ADJUSTABLE SEAT FOR GUNNERS IN ARMED AEROPLANES AND THE LIKE.

APPLICATION FILED AUG. 14, 1917.

1,275,624.

Patented Aug. 13, 1918.

Fig.1.

Fig.2.

INVENTOR.

T. O. M. Sopwith.

By

Attorney.

This patent describes a gunner's seat mounting system that allows the seat to be swiveled for optimum efficiency given the shape/size of a given gunner. It features an "eccentric" or off-center mounting plate that allows the seat to be rotated accordingly.

T. SOPWITH.
BRAKE FOR AEROPLANES.
APPLICATION FILED MAY 12, 1917.

1,293,228.

Patented Feb. 4, 1919.
2 SHEETS—SHEET 1.

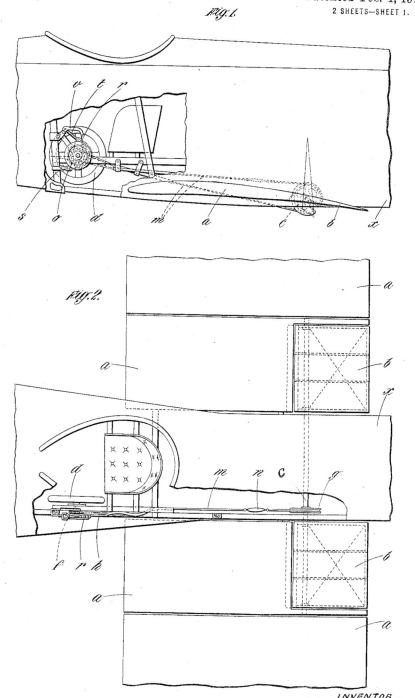

This patent describes the air-brake used on the 1 ½ Strutter. It was essentially a small flap near the wing root of the lower wing, that was actuated by a hand wheel in the cockpit to a variety of degrees—from 0 to 90. It slowed the aircraft on landings giving the pilot more time to make his landing, and allowed a shorter roll-out of same.

INVENTOR
Thomas Sopwith
Per Robert F. Phillips
Attorney.

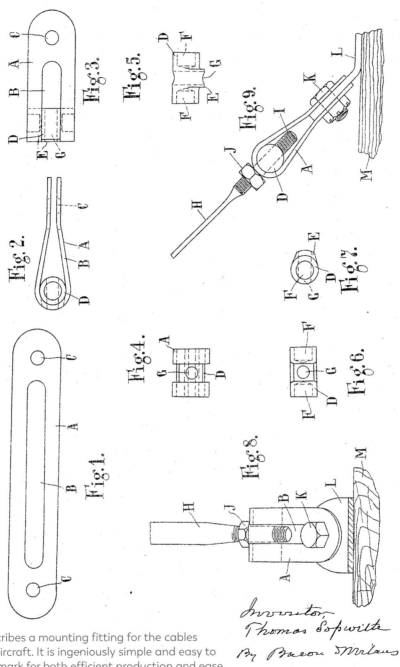

T. SOPWITH.
DEVICE FOR THE ATTACHMENT OF CABLES, WIRES, AND THE LIKE UPON AIRCRAFT.
APPLICATION FILED JULY 7, 1917.

1,299,049.

Patented Apr. 1, 1919.

Inventor,
Thomas Sopwith
By Mason Merlons

This patent describes a mounting fitting for the cables that rigged an aircraft. It is ingeniously simple and easy to fabricate; a hallmark for both efficient production and ease of installation. It consists of a stamped piece of steel that sandwiches a threaded trunnion pin to which the rigging cable is then threaded. The two ends of the stamping are bent around this pin and brought together such that the holes bored in either end line up and then sandwich a mounting tang, and are secured with a bolt (see figures)

| Notes

Introduction

1   C. P. Hill, *British Social and Economic History 1700–1975 – Fourth edition*, p. 236.

2   Ibid.

3   Ibid, p. 237.

4   Graham Wallace, *Flying Witness: Harry Harper and the Golden Age of Aviation*, p. 52.

5   Ibid, p. 123.

6   Robert Wohl, *A Passion for Wings: Aviation and the Western Imagination 1908-1918*, p. 59.

7   Alfred Gollin, *The Impact of Air Power on the British People and their Government, 1909-14*, pp. 76–88.

8   Wohl, p. 38.

9   S. W. Roskill (Editor), *Documents Relating to the Naval Air Service: Vol.1 1908-1918*, p. 156.

10 Wohl, p. 18.

11 Cecil Lewis, *Sagittarius Rising* (London: Peter Davies, 1936), p. 116.

12 *Flight*, April 5, 1917, pp. 321–22.

13 *Flight*, January 20, 1916, pp. 66–67.

14 Hill, p. 240. Women had to be over 30 to vote however, and either the woman voter or her husband had to own or occupy property of an annual value of at least £5.

15 Ibid, p. 239.

16 Ibid, p. 240.

The British Aircraft Industry

17 Hill, p. 238. See Appendix 1 for amplification of the Defence of Realm Act.

18 *Flight*, April 5, 1917, p. 321.

19 *Flight*, October 23, 1914, p. 1060.

20 Grover Loening, *Flight*, January 11, 1917, p. 47.

21 Stepney Blakeney, *How an Aeroplane is Built* (London: "Aeroplane" & General Publishing Co., Ltd., 1918), p. 21.

22 Ibid, p. 29.

23 Ibid, pp. 35–36.

24 Ibid, p. 37.

25 Ibid, p. 44.

26 Ibid, p. 58. The "turn buttons" are teardrop shaped lozenges of ply or solid stock that pivot on an off-center fastener, thus as they rotate they come to bear on the stock and prevent it from moving (see illustration).

27 Ibid, p. 59.

28 Ibid, p. 60.

29 Ibid, p. 62.

30 Ibid, pp. 67–8.

The British and Colonial Aeroplane Company, Ltd (B&CAC) / Bristol

31 David Bremner, *Bristol Scout 1264: Rebuilding Grandad's Aircraft*, p. 34.

32 Ibid, p. 35. B&CAC was created in the Bristol Tramways omnibus depot and repair shop near Bristol. Sir George also created flying schools at Larkhill on Salisbury Plain, and at Brooklands, which was a common business model at the time. Those learning to fly were often on the schools' propriety aircraft (usually of some modification of an existing design).

33 Ibid, p. 16.

34 Ibid.

35 Ibid, p. 22.

36 Ibid, p. 23.

37 Ibid, p. 24.

38 Ibid, p. 25.

39 Ibid.

40 Ibid. p. 27.

41 Ibid, p. 35.

42 Ibid, p. 43.

43 Ibid, p. 62.

44 Ibid, p. 68.

45 Ibid, p. 69. Likely Frank Barnwell was also familiar with the B.S.1 at the Royal Aircraft Factory.

46 Ibid , p. 72.

47 J. M. Bruce, *The Bristol Scouts C & D*, p. 3.

48 Ibid.

49 J. M. Bruce, *The Bristol Scouts C & D*, p. 3.

50 Ibid, p. 5.

51 Ibid, p. 10.

52 Bremner, p. 19. Leo was unhurt save for maybe his pride. The plane was a complete mess and what remained was sent to the UK where it was restored to a non-flying exhibit; it is at the Fleet Air Arm Museum to this day hanging from the ceiling.

53 J. M. Bruce, *The Bristol M.1*, p. 3

54 Ibid.

55 Ibid, p. 4.

56 Ibid, p. 4.

57 Ibid.

58 Ibid, p. 6.

59   Ibid.
60   J. M. Bruce, *The Bristol Fighter*, p. 3.
61   Wally Batter, "The F.2B," *WWI Aero*, no. 74, 1979, p. 28.
62   Ibid.
63   Ibid, p. 29.
64   J. M. Bruce, *The Bristol Fighter*, p. 3.
65   Ibid, p. 4.
66   Ibid.

The Royal Aircraft Factory

67   Nick Garton, *Royal Aircraft Factory S.E.5: 1916 onwards (S.E.5, S.E.5a, S.E.5b & SE-5E Owner's Workshop Manual* p. 10.
68   J. M. Bruce, *The B.E.2, 2a & 2b*, p. 3.
69   Ibid.
70   Ibid, p. 4.
71   Ibid, p. 5.
72   Ibid, p. 6.
73   Ibid.
74   Ibid, p. 7.
75   Ibid, p. 9.
76   Ibid.
77   Ibid, p. 11.
78   Ibid.
79   Garton, p. 12.
80   Ibid.
81   A committee set up by British leadership to investigate the state of British aircraft design and production in response to grave and mounting casualties.
82   Garton, pp. 12–13.
83   Ibid, p. 13.
84   Garton, p. 21.
85   Ibid.
86   Ibid.
87   Garton, p. 22.
88   Garton, p. 22.
89   Garton, p. 13.
90   Ibid, p. 17.
91   Garton, p. 18.
92   Ibid.
93   Ibid.
94   Garton, p. 19.
95   Garton, p. 23.
96   Ibid.
97   Ibid, p. 24.
98   Ibid.
99   Ibid, p. 70.
100 Ibid.
101 Ibid, p. 71.
102 Ibid, p. 72.
103 Ibid.
104 Aircraft Design Notebook of H. P. Folland while serving at the Royal Aircraft Factory from 1912–1916, book number 4 (set of 4 books in all), p. 6.
105 Ibid, p. 76.
106 Ibid, p. 77.
107 Ibid, p. 26.
108 Ibid, p. 28.
109 Ibid, p. 29.
110 Ibid.
111 Ibid.
112 Ibid, p. 30.
113 Ibid.
114 Ibid, p. 78.
115 Bill Lambert, *Combat Report* (London: William Kimber, 1973).
116 Folland's notebook, p. 78. PC stood for "Protective Covering."
117 Ibid, p. 79.

Aircraft Manufacturing Company (Airco)

118 James F. Miller, *DH2 vs Albatros DI/DII* (London: Osprey Publications, 2012), p. 10.
119 Ibid, p. 11.
120 Ibid.
121 J. M. Bruce, *The De Havilland D.H.2.*, p. 3.
122 Harald Penrose, *British Aviation: the Pioneer Years 1903–1914*, p. 246.
123 Ibid. This would be the configuration of throttle and 3 axis control for decades to follow.
124 J. M. Bruce, *The De Havilland D.H.2.*, p. 3.
125 Ibid. An order was placed for 100 DH 1s however.
126 J. M. Bruce, *The De Havilland D.H.2.*, p. 7. Hawker devised a spring clip which allowed the gun to be fired in a fixed, forward position, yet could be released to swivel if need be; at best an unhappy compromise between combat tactics and theoretical dogma espoused by office-bound leadership.
127 Ibid, p. 10.
128 *Flight*, October 24, 1918, p. 1189.
129 J. M. Bruce, *The De Havilland D.H.5*, p. 3.
130 Ibid, p. 5.
131 *Flight*, October 24, 1918, p. 1189.
132 Ibid.
133 Ibid.

134 Ibid.

135 Ibid, p. 1190.

136 Bruce, *The De Havilland D.H.5*, p. 3.

137 Ibid, p. 4

138 Ibid, p. 4.

139 Ibid, p. 5.

140 RAF Museum website, https://www.rafmuseum.org.uk/.

A. V. Roe & Company (Avro)

141 Penrose, p. 70.

142 Ibid, p. 71.

143 Ibid.

144 Ibid, p. 71.

145 Ibid.

146 Ibid, p. 81

147 Ibid, p. 93.

148 Ibid, p. 106.

149 Ibid, p. 110.

150 Ibid, p. 111.

151 Ibid, p. 122.

152 Ibid, p. 125.

153 Ibid, p. 130. He had signed statements from the head carpenter and gatekeeper that he made this flight.

154 Ibid, pp. 133–34.

155 Ibid, p. 148.

156 Ibid, p. 149.

157 Ibid, p. 165.

158 Ibid, p. 173.

159 Ibid, p. 174.

160 Ibid, p. 201.

161 Ibid, p. 214.

162 Ibid, p. 222.

163 Ibid. Distance pieces were short sections of wood that joined the upper and lower strips of wood forming the airfoil.

164 Ibid, p. 291.

165 Ibid, p. 292.

166 Ibid, p. 292.

167 Ibid, p. 322.

168 Ibid, p. 323.

169 Ibid, p. 324.

170 Ibid, p. 338

171 Ibid, p. 324.

172 Ibid, p. 443.

173 Ibid.

174 Ibid.

175 Ibid, p. 464.

176 *Flight*, p. 292.

Sopwith Aviation Company

177 Alan Bramson, *Pure Luck: the Authorized biography of Sir Thomas Sopwith*, p. 28.

178 Ibid, p. 29.

179 Ibid, p. 30.

180 Ibid, p. 32.

181 Ibid.

182 Ibid, p. 33.

183 Ibid, p. 47.

184 Ibid.

185 Ibid, p. 53.

186 Ibid, p. 54.

187 Ibid, p. 55.

188 Ibid, p. 57.

189 Ibid, p. 58.

190 Ibid.

191 Ibid, p. 60.

192 Ibid.

193 Ibid, p. 61.

194 Ibid, p. 63.

195 Ibid.

196 Ibid, p. 64.

197 Ibid, p. 65.

198 Ibid.

199 Ibid, pp. 68–9.

200 Ibid, p. 66.

201 Ibid, p. 67.

202 Ibid.

203 Ibid.

204 M. Davis, *Sopwith Aircraft* (Ramsbury: The Crowood Press Ltd., 1999), p. 9.

205 Bramson, p. 68.

206 Ibid, p. 70.

207 Ibid.

208 Ibid, p. 71.

209 Ibid, p. 73.

210 Davis, p. 10.

211 Wallace, p. 257.

212 Bramson, p. 74.

213 Ibid, p. 77.

214 Ibid, p. 78.

215 Ibid, p. 79.

216 Ibid, pp. 79–80.

217 Ibid, p. 80.

218 Davis, p. 10.

219 Bramson, pp. 83–84.

220 Ibid, p. 84.

221 Ibid, p. 85.

222 Ibid, p. 85.

223 Ibid.

224 J. M. Bruce, *The Sopwith 1½ Strutter*, p. 3.

225 Davis, p. 39.

226 J. M. Bruce, *The Sopwith 1½ Strutter*, p. 3.

227 Davis, p. 33.

228 Bramson, p. 91.

229 Ibid, p. 39.

230 Davis, p. 39.

231 Bramson, p. 90.

232 Ibid.

233 Davis, p. 49.

234 The name was given when Col. Sefton Brancker of the War Office visited Brooklands to see the new fighter; the little fighter was standing next to a much large aircraft and the Col. Said "Looks as though it had a pup" and the name stuck. Bramson, p. 87.

235 Mick Davis, *Sopwith Aircraft*, p. 53.

236 J. M. Bruce, *The Sopwith Pup*, p. 3.

237 Ibid, p. 4.

238 Bramson, p. 87.

239 Ibid. p. 88.

240 Davis, *Sopwith Aircraft*, p. 62. James McCudden ordered this done.

241 Bruce, *The Sopwith Pup*, p. 4.

242 Ibid, p. 5.

243 Ibid.

244 Ibid, p. 7.

245 Ibid, p. 11.

246 Bramson, p. 93.

247 At least one triplane was tested with the 110 hp Le Rhône rotary engine with negligible positive results.

248 Clayton & Shuttleworth built six triplanes with twin guns but the increase in weight and subsequent reduction in flight performance marginalized their efficacy.

249 J. M. Bruce, *The Sopwith Triplane*, p. 4.

250 Ibid.

251 Jarrod Cotter, *Sopwith Camel: 1916–20 (F.1/2.F.1) Owner's Workshop Manual*, p. 23.

252 Bramson, p. 94.

253 Ibid, p. 95.

254 *Flight*, September 12, 1918, p. 1019.

255 J. M. Bruce, *The Sopwith F.1 Camel* (Leatherhead: Profile Publications, 1966), p. 3.

256 *Flight*, September 12, 1918, p. 1019.

257 *Flight*, September 12, 1918, p. 1019.

258 Ibid.

259 Ibid.

260 Flight, September 12, 1918, p. 1019.

261 Ibid.

262 Bramson, p. 95.

263 David. K. Vaughan (Editor), *Letters from a War Bird: the World War I Correspondence of Elliott White Springs*, p. 179.

264 Ibid, p. 180.

265 Davis, *Sopwith Aircraft*, p. 95.

266 J. M. Bruce, *The Sopwith Dolphin*, p. 3.

267 J. M. Bruce, *The Sopwith 7F.1 Snipe*, p. 3.

268 Ibid.

269 Ibid, p. 3.

270 Ibid.

Engines and Props

271 *Flight*, October 20, 1921, p. 691.

272 *Flight*, December 14, 1916, p. 1095.

| Bibliography

Batter, Wally. "The F.2B." *WWI Aero*, no. 74, 1979.

Bowyer, Chaz. *The Bristol F.2B*. Leatherhead: Profile Publications, 1967.

Bramson, Alan. *Pure Luck: the authorized biography of Sir Thomas Sopwith*. Manchester: Crécy Publishing Ltd., 2005.

Bremner, David. *Bristol Scout 1264: Rebuilding Grandad's Aircraft*. Stroud: Fonthill Media Ltd., 2018.

Bruce, J. M. *The De Havilland D.H.2*. Leatherhead: Profile Publications, 1966.

Bruce, J. M. *The De Havilland D.H.5*. Leatherhead: Profile Publications, 1967.

Bruce, J. M. *The Bristol Scouts C & D*. Leatherhead: Profile Publications, 1967.

Bruce, J. M. *The Bristol M.1*. Leatherhead: Profile Publications, 1967.

Bruce, J. M. *The B.E.2, 2a & 2b*. Leatherhead: Profile Publications, 1966.

Bruce, J. M. *The Bristol Fighters*. Leatherhead: Profile Publications, 1965.

Bruce, J. M. *The S.E.5*. Leatherhead: Profile Publications, 1966.

Bruce, J. M. *The S.E.5A*. Leatherhead: Profile Publications, 1966.

Bruce, J. M. *The Sopwith Pup*. Leatherhead: Profile Publications, 1965.

Bruce, J. M. *The Sopwith Triplane*. Leatherhead: Profile Publications, 1966.

Bruce, J. M. *The Sopwith Camel F.1*. Leatherhead: Profile Publications, 1966.

Bruce, J. M. *The Sopwith 1½ Strutter*. Leatherhead: Profile Publications, 1966.

Bruce, J. M. *The Sopwith Dolphin*. Leatherhead: Profile Publications, 1967.

Bruce, J. M. *The Sopwith 7F.1 Snipe*. Leatherhead: Profile Publications, 1965.

Cotter, Jarrod. *Sopwith Camel: 1916–20 (F.1/2.F.1) Owner's Workshop Manual*. Sparkford: Haynes Publishing, 2016.

Davis, M. *Sopwith Aircraft*. Ramsbury: The Crowood Press Ltd., 1999.

Garton, Nick. *Royal Aircraft Factory S.E.5, 1916 onwards (S.E.5, S.E.5a, S.E.5b & SE-5E Owner's Workshop Manual)*. Sparkford: Haynes Publishing, 2017.

Golin, Alfred. *The Impact of Air Power on the British People and their Government, 1909–1914*. London: Palgrave Macmillan, 1989.

Hill, C. P. *British Economic and Social History 1700–1975, Fourth edition*. London: Edward Arnold Publishing, 1977.

Miller, James F. *D.H.2 vs. Albatros DI/DII Western Front 1916*. Oxford: Osprey Publishing, 2012.

Penrose, Harald. *British Aviation: the Pioneer Years 1903–1914*. London: Putnam, 1967.

Roskill, S. W. (Editor), *Documents Relating to the Naval Air Service: Vol.1 1908–1918*. London: Navy Records Society, 1970.

Vaughan, David. K. (Editor) *Letters from a War Bird: the World War I Correspondence of Elliott White Springs*. Columbia: University of South Carolina Press, 2012.

Wallace, Graham. *Flying Witness: Harry Harper and the Golden Age of Aviation*. London: Putnam and Co, 1958.

Wohl, Robert. *A Passion for Wings: Aviation and the Western Imagination 1908–1918*. New Haven: Yale University Press, 1994.

| Index